# Spiritual
# Intelligence

# Spiritual Intelligence

## What We Can Learn from the Early Awakening Child

### MARSHA SINETAR

ORBIS BOOKS

Maryknoll, New York 10545

The Catholic Foreign Mission Society of America (Maryknoll) recruits and trains people for overseas missionary service. Through Orbis Books, Maryknoll aims to foster the international dialogue that is essential to mission. The books published, however, reflect the opinions of their authors and are not meant to represent the official position of the society. To obtain more information about Maryknoll or Orbis Books, please visit our website at www.maryknoll.org.

Published in 2000 by
Orbis Books
P.O. Box 308
Maryknoll, New York 10545-0308
U.S.A.

Manufactured in the United States of America

**Library of Congress Cataloging-in-Publication Data**

Sinetar, Marsha.
   Spiritual intelligence : what we can learn from the early awakening child / Marsha Sinetar.
      p.   cm.
   Includes bibliographical references.
   ISBN 1-57075-231-1 (hardcover)
   1. Spiritual life. 2. Experience (Religion) in children.   I. Title.

BL624 .S53435  2000
291.1′783423 – dc21

99-088454

*For friends, far and near:*

*Brother Harold Thibodeau*
Abbey of Gethsemani

*Brother M. René Richie*
Abbey of Gethsemani

*Dianne Molvig*

*Maryruth Wilde*

*I said, Days should speak,*
*and multitude of years should teach wisdom.*
*But there is a spirit in man:*
*and the inspiration of the Almighty*
*giveth them understanding*

JOB 32:7–8


*I have no greater joy than to hear*
*that my children walk in truth.*

3 JOHN 4

# Contents

# Introduction

Spiritual intelligence is inspired thought. It is light, the kiss of life that awakens our sleeping beauty. It animates people of any age, in any situation. In children, that quickening makes boys and girls want to seek out and cultivate their inborn gifts, energies, and desires. This book says let's stay open to that kiss of life. Let's trust in its existence. And more: I say that certain blessed children display such hunger for some sacred idea or truth burning within that they, or at least selected patterns of behavior, can be guides. The young can show us how to express our own spiritual truths. In a nutshell that's what this book is about.

In the Book of Mark (12:34) we read that when a certain scribe revealed a deep inner knowing, Jesus of Nazareth said he was nearing the kingdom of God. That scribe was inspired. He had "spiritual intelligence," the heightened discernment that we often say generates supernatural qualities: intuition, a firm moral compass, power or inner authority, the ability to discern right from wrong, and wisdom. Some children are on fire with such traits, and each chapter explores these qualities.

Decades ago, the rather worldly psychiatrist R. D. Laing acknowledged that "each child is a new being, a potential prophet, a new spiritual prince [or princess], a new spark of light precipitating into the outer darkness."[1]

A few children express a brightness I call *early awakening:* Inspired thought or spiritual intelligence leads some youngsters to a superior understanding of themselves. Faithful to an inner beat, they reject anyone, or anything, that weakens it. That awakening approaches the illumination long held by the mystical tradition to signify the truth that sets free. This is, as St. Teresa of Avila said, "a union of love with love" and so subtle and delicate "there is no way of describing" its operations.[2]

Much like the scribe deemed intelligent by Jesus, these children make contact with their intuitional depths sooner than others. Their excitement intensifies. They may be superperceptive. May comprehend the large issues of life. May exceed the mastery of mere mechanical prowess (such as playing the piano well or earning top grades). They'll gravitate toward life-paths that reflect the nobility of who they are. Their inspired thoughts motivate and ignite optimism — even in the face of obstacles. Why is this? This book is driven by that question. In other words, what attributes do children with high spiritual intelligence share? And how do those attributes influence adults?

To answer, I'll explore a mix of traits that prepare children for an entire life of self-respect and creative contribution. Writing as an educator, and sometimes personally — but not as a parent or a therapist — I'll suggest why early awakeners flourish in the face of challenge while others shut down, ignore, or reject their life-affirming thoughts.

Early awakeners see things that aren't as though they were. All of us are born with the potential to actualize what psychologist Abraham Maslow called the Being-values — joy, courage, creativity, compassion, and the like. Since it's been estimated that somewhere around 10 percent of adults adopt a self-actualizing development process, I suggest that even in childhood most such people make conscious choices to cultivate that seed of life.

My clearest portrayals of spiritual intelligence come from interviewing accomplished adults. For the past twenty years, as the head of a small corporate and leadership-development firm, I have chosen to work with inventive, productive adults. My clients' thought processes are vivid and pronounced. Many are world-class, innovative thinkers. Most function in the senior management ranks of thriving twenty-first-century corporations. In these pages, I look to the ground of youth that seems to enable the mature success. As creative adults describe their childhoods, it's obvious that a spiritual fomenting — inspired thought — has animated their particular motifs of being. This is true of children too. They're not *trying* to be inspired. They are being inspired, quickened, superbly motivated, and, somehow, protected from within. To support that thesis I've provided stories of youngsters who transcend difficulty in order to "walk in truth" — not as a cool, clinical view of the topic, but as a montage and a creative synthesis I've been assembling over the course of my professional life. Throughout are offered snippets of heartfelt ideas put to me by high-schoolers with whom I've conversed. Years of work in the public school system, as delineated in chapter 1, contributed enormously to this book, and I've also shared selected Kodak-moments from my own youth's journey that I hope illustrate the stirrings of abundant life so many of us felt in childhood and feel now. An understanding of spiritual intelligence sheds light on how we become our own best selves, while suggesting ways to improve our service to the lives of all children.

Loving, responsible commitment to the spiritual variables of child-rearing is a holy function. Human beings are God's "first fruits," and in our Good Shepherd's role, we're not asked to "fix" children or make them spiritual according to some expert's ten-step plan. We're simply to protect and respect the young, to mentor them as caring stewards while we live from an inspired, competent, and wholesome base ourselves. Regarding spiritual intelligence, I bend the old saw, "It takes one to know one," to "It takes one to develop one."

## Dialogue to Nurture Wisdom

Childhood is not simply a lark. It is a season of rehearsal for roles and traits best-suited to each individual. Early awakeners prepare for distinctive paths sensing the part they are destined to play on life's stage. That knowing gives them a head start on genuineness.

Understanding authenticity or wisdom in children can guide us through our own authentic pilgrimage as adults. The same elements that dampen youngsters' vital life dampen ours. Raising our awareness about wisdom means entering into a dialogue about what constitutes, furthers, or blunts spiritual intelligence. This book raises more questions than it answers: What does it mean to possess an illumined mind? How do we achieve "right relationship" with ourselves? What threats to inspired thinking predictably try to undermine us? How do children and how do we really forgive injustices? For answers, the integrities of our soul demand attention.

As we'll see in chapter 1, we must not suppose that if we or our children are not overtly "holy," not all awash with stereotypical spiritual sentiment, that it's too late to cultivate compassion, an enhanced aesthetic, or harmony. That ship sails daily. Momentarily. Here and now anyone, at any age, can hop on board and push out into the deep waters.

## Overview of Terms and a "Right Mind"

This is a book about consciousness, not psychology. Spiritual intelligence involves the animation of inmost truth. It's the bringing to life of what is best and whole and most fully human within. Ideas, energy, values, vision, drive, and vocational directions all flow from within, from a state of awareness alive with love.

In these chapters I'll emphasize and discuss:

- spiritual intelligence within a general context of creative giftedness,
- the unique projections, or archetypes, that surround many spiritually intelligent youngsters,
- the inner traits that boost children's wisdom, for example, the ability to daydream freely, to use solitary pursuits, and to protest productively,
- the cultivation of these qualities in adulthood.

All chapters explore the challenge of providing youngsters with a positive spiritual foundation. All suggest specific benefits that adults might gain from observing and understanding the dynamics of early awakeners.

Chapter 1's overview proposes that whatever else might influence children, by about age ten (in many cases much sooner) the live wires lean on three decidedly spiritual, intuitional strengths:

- an inner authority,
- singleminded interests,
- discernment of a spiritual idea — or whole ideal — that enlivens them.

In early awakeners, such attributes coalesce productively. Instinctive youngsters are acutely receptive to inner cues. They are animated at the root — at their very essence. They are self-respecting. Early capability and wholesome choices, not necessarily easy circumstances, good grades or "good feelings," raise self-worth. Early awakeners' conscious choices tend to work. These are effective, constructive girls and boys who enjoy getting things done and done well. And we learn that sheer competence can produce lasting self-respect.

These children pass practical tests: Only in their "right mind" — integrated and spiritually aware — do they graduate to a degree of wit that, like in fairy tales, destroys witches and wolves or transcends other looming threats. Pluck, optimism, faith, constructive action, even agility in the face of danger and difficulty — all these are spiritual traits. Let us also remember Baltasar Gracián's sagacity:

> Virtue is a chain of perfections, the center of all happiness. She makes you prudent, discreet, shrewd, sensible, wise, honest, happy, praiseworthy, true ... a universal hero.[3]

Youngsters can, and regularly do, save their own skins. Youth is the time for the thoughtful gestation of every sort of necessary trait and skill.

Pursuing such themes I worked "against type," searching out stories of young people that dismantle our narrow stereotypes of childhood. As noted, I share snapshots, not an album of the whole life. A single image can make spiritual intelligence comprehensible. Although someone's later years may be flawed or neurotic, these early images depict the concrete promise and serve as a model of the blessedness we all crave. I have a soft spot for boys and girls who make sweet lemonade out of sour lemons, who translate negative experience into a positive, spiritual reality, or who cling tenaciously to their truths. They may endure untold anxieties to follow meaningful purposes. They evade the intrusions of others: parents, teachers, or society. That's fortunate, since adults can and do get in the way of a child's sacred unfolding.

I'll give no tips on the repair or doctoring-up of youngsters. Children, I contend, come to us with an intrinsic seed of wisdom ready-made and whole. As Scripture promises, "the seed is in itself" (Gen. 1:11–12).

Timeless spiritual principles, not quick-fix ploys, nurture that seed of wisdom, encouraging the healthy growth of intuition and inspired thought. For instance, we can provide children and ourselves with a home, school, and community climate that breeds emotional safety. I'll stress this repeatedly. Left unchecked, emotional trauma can degrade vital life. False loyalties take the edge off our courage, self-respect, and even spiritual intelligence. When we're inspired we see life through a framework of inspiration; when traumatized we see through our traumas.

I'll repeat one rule: *We adults teach what we are being.* A child's intuition is a radar that homes in on the adult's turn of mind, our *inner* stance. If we utter loving words but inside ourselves are a boiling cauldron of hostility, they'll hear our rage. If we're trusting, chances are they'll learn to trust. A child's self-view, belief-system, and habits are cultivated one infinitesimal imprint at a time, like ours. Another reiterated point: Spiritual intelligence is linked to, yet transcends, what we typically consider *religious* predilection.

People of every age and type tell me that they *need* to cultivate their own spirituality, unity, completeness, and well-lived truths. Desire like that moves us beyond constraints and hardship. It's even said that sound mental health involves knowing what's true for us and being able to articulate that. In our heart of hearts, each of us longs to know who we are and to be that, to live that reality. Goethe observed, "All human longing is a longing for God." Early awakeners reinforce that message.

Understanding spiritual intelligence in children helps us understand ourselves, for early awakening is more than a metaphor for our deepest aspirations. The seed of promise we felt in youth still lives at our own core. Not age alone but the inspirations of the Almighty giveth us understanding.

# Chapter One

# Inspired Thought

*I'm imaginative, a bookworm, inventive, and complex. Isn't everyone? I'm also a nature lover, sensitive, quiet, and empathic — questioning and inquisitive.* — Student, age sixteen

At four years of age, Aimee Semple McPherson, the charismatic evangelist and healer, could "stand on a drumhead on the street corner and draw a crowd by reciting the best Bible stories."[1] Aimee was mischievous, not blemish-free, no Goodie-Two-Shoes. Yet even as a preschooler her inherent leadership talent and disposition were clear. She possessed an innate ability to influence others and sophisticated communication skills. These gifts called Aimee to life, inspired her thought, and gave her an intuitive authority.

Yvette Glover, mother of tap-dancing prodigy and Tony award winner Savion Glover, told an interviewer:

Even before [my son] was born, I just knew something was up. He had terrific rhythm at a very early age, as a baby.... He would go into my cupboard, into where my pots and pans were, and he would take them all out on the floor and just start beating on them.[2]

9

By age four, Savion Glover was playing drums and tap dancing. At twelve, he was starring in *The Tap Dance* on Broadway. Yvette Glover, like many mothers, may have sensed a distinctive type of individual in her womb during pregnancy. Spiritual intelligence furthered the uniqueness of her child's infancy, early years, adolescence, and beyond.

## Overview: Inspired Thought

Philosopher Albert Camus contended that all of us, "above a certain elementary level of consciousness," seek rules, formulas, or attitudes for the integration we lack. We sense a better world and chase it. But "better does not mean different, it means unified."[3] Further, the passion which lifts us above the commonplace is born of an inspired, intuitive authority that tells us unity is our birthright.

My bias is simple: The advancement toward wholeness is grounded in the stuff of youth. Or, I should say in the instinctual life of spiritually intelligent children. The girls and boys I call early awakeners demonstrate an authority for the integration that is theirs alone. That idea of oneness, that passion for unity is a keynote of spiritual intelligence. Since coming to an awareness of the oneness of life is the business of life, there is much we can learn from early awakeners.

These lively, creative children can tire us out with their flights of fancy, their ardors, their focused energy. For better or worse, their laser-like purposefulness *is* the seeking of unity that is spiritual. It's also what we call wisdom. That wisdom may not make anyone smarter in school, in work, or in friendships. It could impede. Borrowing from an old Yiddish proverb, the wise tend to hear one word and understand two. All passionate minds work overtime, but not necessarily along orthodox lines. Spiritual intelligence is, in essence, synonymous with that focused passion and confounding wisdom.

Heightened awareness lets some children reach beyond expected norms or limits, toward what a colleague called a "rich religious imagination." Others might say these girls and boys crave the transcendence that mystics extol.

### Little "Old Souls"

Throughout history children with strong spiritual drives have displayed a zeal for independence. They also embody compassionate ideals and "Being-values": joy, humor, inventiveness, beauty, truthfulness. The records of the lives of protégés, gifted leaders, and saintly types prove they frequently began, in early childhood and quite consciously and concretely, to "tend their Father's business." Let us once and for all reduce to absurdity the popular, simplistic notion that all girls and boys inhabit a fuzzy, somnambulistic state of mind until some magical coming-of-age in adulthood. Or that every child's bid for autonomy is simply a stubborn rebellion against authority.

Each child is unique. True, many children do need strict and careful overseeing. Many don't. Many children are wise, little old souls, a fact parents routinely observed and acknowledged as early as the eleventh century when themes of the "old child" were documented in accounts from Germany, France, and Italy:

The old child avoids the company of other children, preferring solitude. He does not play games, engage in horseplay or tell or listen to dirty stories. He does not indulge in what [is referred to] as the common sensuality of ordinary children. The old child studies hard, prays regularly, and attends church gladly.[4]

I do not contend every flash of inspiration makes every child an "old soul." I do claim that many children, perhaps the majority, know their own mind. They understand goodness or virtue, and can be trusted to sense what is best for them. And more: Such knowledge serves them well. It cultivates self-respect and a fine, firm grip on reality.

In my observation, the spiritually intelligent do not shut off their gusto for life as they mature. They may possess neuroticisms — even the saintly can seem like odd ducks to onlookers. Nevertheless, their self- and worldview, or perceptual stance, instructs. For the spiritually intelligent, the unitive consciousness, or sense of oneness with the sacred, exists here and now within the realm of everyday life even with its turmoil. The unitive identification lets us see what's possible — the holy ideal — despite the cracks and smudges of what exists (see the chart on the facing page). Who are these early awakening youngsters? How do I happen to write of them? To answer, I share some personal background.

## Personal Patterns

I began my professional life as a classroom teacher and quickly developed an affinity for teaching creative, gifted

## CHARACTERISTICS OF
## SPIRITUALLY INTELLIGENT CHILDREN

In youth, the spiritually intelligent share many qualities, not all equally evident in every child. We learn from observing young people that the chief characteristics of heightened consciousness are related to a perception of unity and include:

- *Acute self-awareness, intuition, the "I am"- power* or built-in authority.

- *Broad worldview:* see self and others as interrelated; realize without being taught that the cosmos is somehow alive and shining; possess what has been termed "subjective light."[5]

- *Moral elevation, strong opinions, a tendency to experience delight,* "peak-experiences," and/or aesthetic preferences.

- *An understanding of where they're headed:* have a sense of destiny; see the possible (i.e., the holy or whole ideal) in the midst of the mundane.

- *"Unappeasable hunger"[6] for selective interests,* often prompting solitary or single-minded pursuits; generally altruistic or want to contribute to others.

- *Fresh, "weird" notions; well-developed humor:* We ask such youngsters, "Where do you get these ideas?" and wonder if these aren't ancient souls in young bodies.

- *Pragmatic, efficient perception of reality,* which often (but not always) produces healthy choices and practical results.[7]

youngsters. Later, as a public school principal and before opening my own firm, I designed and supervised programs for every sort of student with special needs: the "learning handicapped," the early childhood pupil, the gifted. As I wrote in *The Mentor's Spirit*, especially in the primary grades I found spiritual vitality everywhere. Each child seemed inspired — eager to express the truth, beauty, and integrity felt within. Each reminded me of facets of myself I'd walled off due to childhood losses. The school I headed up became a teacher-training site for local universities and a demonstration center for innovative educational methods, including pilot programs for what were then, in California, called Mentally Gifted Minors. That diagnostic catch-all phrase was meant to encompass both the academically and the creatively gifted.

In a few years, I was asked to design curriculums and assess courses of study for local, county, and state programs — again, primarily for students with strong academic or inventive talents. Every child has "early awakening" potential. In the unbounded universe of giftedness, academic and creative talent are two distinct categories, but not always exclusive of one another. Barring overlaps between these two types, the highly creative appear to take life's marching orders from within.

## Academic vs. Creative Talent

The *academically* talented earn good grades. They usually gain entrance to advanced placement courses. Score top marks on their SATs. Form the backbone of most Ivy League student bodies. Of course they can be extraordinarily inventive, yet they tend to behave swimmingly.

That conduct sets them apart. Smart in their studies and socially adroit, these young people incline toward well-roundedness. They tuck in their shirttails and aren't prone to stud their body parts with gold pins and diamond beads. Look at the school record of most administrators or finance chiefs and you'll probably find academic talent. Now to some extent we are all spiritually intelligent. It's just that in too many of us some sparkle has dulled. Ardor has cooled. The signs of inspiration, animation, the quickening from within are tougher to spot. But we can rekindle the flame.

The *creatively* gifted are incandescent — original, quirky, resourceful sorts. They contribute to the greater good, but always in their own way and time. Even when they're inward, we notice in their eyes a sparkle of vivid *animation*. A deeper mind stirs them to life. Since the early 1980s, I've called that thought process "spiritually intelligent" because it sparks vitality and useful ideas, "brings insight, ability, an unrelenting wish to make sense of [inner] cues: Love, longing, feelings of gratefulness, the need to serve or relinquish the familiar for the unknown."[8]

The *spiritually* intelligent comprise our world's most novel thinkers. Look at the childhoods of Nobel Peace Prize winners — like Nelson Mandela or Aung San Suu Kyi. You'll spot early patterns of virtue, goodness, empathy, and fair play. And their imaginations are alive with the presence of ideals that, at some point, become concretely manifest. The leadership power is evident, even in youth. Some of these youngsters make waves at an early age. No judgments, please: We're not talking "better." We're talking different. Divergent. Youngsters who stray from the norms of the pack. Early awakeners often reject The Party Line, frequently neglecting what we adults value to pursue what they love.

They could find their class work so boring that they poorly tolerate school. Conventional studies may weary and frustrate them. (Not always.) Peers and family members may misunderstand their most basic emotional needs. These children might strike out on standardized tests. (I once watched one blithe six-year-old connect all the answer-dots on his multiple choice form and another blacken in every computerized response-bubble on her IQ test.) As scholars, they could just get by. Or drop out of formal schooling too soon for our comfort. Or drift about aimlessly for a spell. Or join the Peace Corps. Or hitchhike through Europe after high school, like overheated nomads panting for a drink of pure self-knowledge before settling down to what *we* call life's traditional business. In sum: Each early awakener is a minority of one. They think "outside the box" because they *are* outside the box.

No single size, shape, or rule of conduct fits all. Some personify a pristine innocence: Lofty ideals fairly ooze from their cerebral pores. Others of these dear sons and daughters tempt fate: They not only smoke, they inhale. There's a jazz within, an offbeat rhythm, and they're listening to that. Not to us. In other words, like Aimee Semple McPherson, our most inventive, inspired progeny are not automatically angelic types. "Honor thy father and mother..." reads one great Commandment. In these pages you'll meet youngsters who rarely obey that mandate — or any other — legalistically. Yet they're faithful to the *spirit* of good. By a graceful synthesis that knows self and other as Self, these children venerate life as one sparkling whole, as if they're sighing along with mystic Meister Eckhart, "my eye and God's eye, that is one eye and one vision, one knowledge and one love."[9]

## What Is Spiritual Intelligence?

Spiritual intelligence is inspired thought. It's inspired drive and effectiveness, the "is-ness" or aliveness of divinity of which we're all a part. "God" is my word of choice for the source of that fervor: "unoriginated, immutable, eternal, self-sustained existence and creative power."[10] Some people may prefer other language. When consummate sculptress Louise Nevelson described her girlhood's drive, she used her own words, not terms like "spiritual intelligence" or "vocation." But we feel her exhilaration, her long-range plans, her heart's exalted intent:

> Some of us, even when we were little children, wanted something else — what life really gives. Something that would justify our being here. And I meant it. And I would take nothing else.[11]

That yearning or love for what life really gives *is* the seeking of unity that St. Augustine said apprehends eternal things. I used to believe that if only certain psychological basics — like high self-esteem — were cultivated, our mind would automatically transcend its limits and apprehend eternal things. Now I'd say not necessarily. After reading about the youthful years of inspired contributors — Maya Angelou, John Muir, Dag Hammarskjöld, to name but three — I'd say it all depends. Now I'd have to agree with John 3:6–8: "That which is born of Spirit is spirit" and, like the wind, it

bloweth where it listeth, and thou hearest the sound
thereof, but canst not tell whence it cometh, and
whither it goeth: So is every one that is born of the
Spirit.

Early awakeners "bloweth where the Spirit listeth."
They are loyal to their spiritual core. Sensing an authentic
presence or some irresistible idea within their consciousness, or heart, they long for and move in the direction
of whatever will ripen its unique expressions. As we
heard from Louise Nevelson, that heightened awareness
bestows vital purpose. That's why early awakeners seem
destined — obliged — to refine their gifts. Heartache and
hardship may force their hand. Usually, the sheer joy of
exploring the potentials of their own talent is impetus
enough to motivate the struggle toward a private aesthetic
or mastery in some chosen field. To me, that struggle is
devotional, its sacred quest rooted in a sense of who one
is, at the core.

## What Is "Spiritual"?

In principle, the word "spiritual" is a neutral term. Simply because people look angelic does not automatically
mean they teem with what Scripture terms "fruits of the
Spirit": hope, faith, charity, patience or divine illumination. One could be other-worldly along seemingly devilish
lines, immersed in dark phantasms. That possibility aside,
I'll emphasize the conventional usage, the one implied by
the morally elevated everywhere when they use the term
"spiritual": divine; animated essence; virtuous; a quality
or attribute of consciousness that reflects what, earlier,

was called the Being-values. And let's not overcomplicate this, either.

Young preschoolers, listening to bedtime stories, get it: Goodness enhances life. It is akin to gladness, the soul's own song. As a colleague's six-year-old daughter wrote so tenderly in her Disney Princess diary:

> When I grow up I want to be a saint or an Angel. I still like booda too but I wish I could see him. I feel nice, not grouchy and I'm not mean to anyone. I be good so my parents don't be mad and I don't watch that much TV.
>
> Booda and Jesus our here for me. Goodness leads to God. My sister might think that being good makes you an Angel but I think God and everyone makes sure that I'm an Angel in my own way.

The timeless heart of childhood understands that wit and virtue make for happy endings, and inspired youngsters figure out, without directly being told, what the word "spiritual" involves. One woman remembered: "My parents were agnostic. Even without their blessings, as a young girl I knew that where spirituality exists, there is no division, no barrier. Reverence toward life is intrinsic to the spiritual person's character."

Reverence for life stimulates an irrepressible drive to honor life. Some early awakeners vow loyalty to their deepest vocational passions. They sign up, as it were, in adolescence for lifelong service to art, law, medicine, or God. Or seem ripe to actualize a *specific* destiny. Thus to my Introduction's question ("What traits cause some children to be so intensely passionate and eventually so productive?"), I find one lavish answer: It's love. By this,

I don't mean sentiment or even familial affection. I mean love as a surrendered quest for unity or Oneness. The transition, or growth, to the integrity of who one is means a loving identification with universal values and *greater* individuality, not a loss of identity. That love manifests distinctive insight, compassion, vigor, and infinitely lovely or useful ideas. *That* love brings one to life. Fixes thought and heart on superordinate goals. Only that love never fails (1 Cor. 13).

Inspired thought processes, expressed humanly, produce inner direction and all that that authority implies in terms of conduct. Decades before the so-called midlife crises and far ahead of their peers, some children exhibit a blessed development. They get excited about something specific — music or color or their butterfly collections. They're turned on by a progressive, healthy independence, and not necessarily because of a nurturing environment. What turns them on and toward wholeness is the sweet guest living within.

## Growing Whole

Early awakeners are flamingly themselves. They're spiritually intelligent because their thoughts and choices integrate all the fragmenting pulls that, in others, seem contradictory. If that wholeness means anything, it means *complete* — not "perfect" (as in blemish-free). Certainly not "finished" (as in over and done with). Completeness means the progressive unfolding of the gauzy, dazzling variables of self-realization.

Psychiatrist A. Reza Arasteh called wholeness "final integration": a transcultural, transcendent state. Psycho-

logical wholeness is born of spiritual unity. It is linked
to holiness. To the extent *we,* and *our* children, become
whole, we — and our children — feel capable, worthwhile, genuine, ready to express our truest ideas. We
pull out the stops and encounter each delicious moment.
That progression is spiritually bright. Inspired. Something
within catches on fire, is alive with intelligible purpose.

Each child is potentially unfolding a seed of pure integrity and power. Jesus of Nazareth taught that the
Kingdom of Heaven lives within. The renowned Hindu
poet Kabir wrote that until we have found God within —
in our own soul — our life will be empty and meaningless.
People all over the planet feel that sacred interior state
provides everything. Universally, it is accepted as divine.

## Progressive Spiritual Unfolding

You may identify with this: A heart attack, a near-death
episode, a love affair, the birth of your child, or an impending retirement wakes you up, shakes you up, alerts
you to lost dreams or your mortality. Reminds you how
much you love life. Then you step lively, reject your
false gods of money, status, or familiar routine and admit who you really are. You surrender to life. That choice
frees you to accept the consequences of seeking solitude,
or marriage, or revising your novel for the umpteenth
time. Or you take a long-overdue moratorium from a
spirit-draining job. You say goodbye to hypocritical relationships. Reflectively, you cast about this way and that,
hoping through trial and error to quench your thirst
for life-meaning or for God. In every form the bid for
wholeness seeks to express an electric, life-affirming love.

Most of us have, at some point, experienced this transformational impulse. Or we've watched it consume someone we know. I merely add that certain extraordinary children — the live wires — act like mature seekers. In youth they are feverish for some sacrosanct purpose, already eager for what's called a "second birth." They know primordial truths live deep within the tributaries of their soul. What's more, their awareness directs us to the tasks of our own growth.

The call to wholeness is enormously stimulating. Consider boys and girls who taste in some new learning their new freedom. Author Annie Dillard tells us that, for her, reading a book of fiction in childhood "was a bomb...a land mine you wanted to go off. You wanted it to blow your whole day."[12] Children's writer Roald Dahl says he got a huge charge out of simply riding a bike:

> I can remember very clearly the journeys I made to and from the school because they were so tremendously exciting. Great excitement is probably the only thing that really interests a six-year-old boy and it sticks in his mind.... I rode to school on [my tricycle] every day with my eldest sister riding on hers. No grown-ups came with us, and I can remember oh so vividly how the two of us used to go racing at enormous tricycle speeds down the middle of the road and then, most glorious of all, when we came to a corner, we would lean to one side and take it on two wheels.[13]

Haven't we all occasionally been excited by the prod of adventure and greater life? Haven't we known some youngster such as I'm describing, called him or her "an old soul," or "wise beyond years"? Even Dr. Arasteh, who mainly studied exceptional, self-realizing adults, admitted that within certain children resides a "master-adult seeking to unfold his or her true self."[14]

## Playful Solitude

Spiritually intelligent children ponder the mysteries of existence. For that pondering, they covet solitude. Or they'll use privacy to immerse themselves in favorite activities. They read. They draw. They stare at walls. They listen to music, dance, go fishing, or toy endlessly with what some consider mind-numbing computer games. In these fanciful hours, there is learning going on. Play is productive. It's the chief employer of childhood. (One hardly knows what to make of "cult of efficiency" schools — and Boards of Education — that now have schemes for less recess, or none at all.)[15]

Critical treasures of intelligence develop during a child's daydreamy processes and make-believe. An enriched inner life, fantasy, the projections of a pretend world prepare youngsters for life. Adults who appropriately encourage the charms of such play encourage children to wholeness. Infancy is not too soon to notice what a baby wants or prefers. And adulthood is not too late to heed what we love, either.

Play's the thing. Play unlocks talent and frees up thinking. Rather than providing an escape hatch from reality (as some rigid adults view a child's imaginary life), freely chosen, frequently isolated, self-styled amusements develop intelligence. Play draws children out. It lets them know themselves and be real. Play is youth's master teacher. It opens doors to what a child may sense is a preexisting order, as one writer explained:

> When I was four, I'd sit at the piano, make up little songs and sing for hours. Or, I'd put on music and with my arms spread to the sky, fly with abandon around the room, totally in private.... My exuberance was personal, nothing I'd ever seen anyone else do, some way of being I'd always known.

If you are an aware, creative child, you'll be immersed in such discovery. Play *is* your "work." It's how you explore the tone and terrain of your inmost landscape, your ground of being. Play helps you relate to your world at large and easily consumes all your time.

Educator Grace Pilon proposes that the awareness of one's power to do things independently brings joy and peace of mind.[16] We encourage children's wisdom, direction, and harmony by giving them ample opportunities to shape their own play, to do as much as they safely can on their own. That independence has a subtle downside: A youngster's favorite pastimes could subvert and discount a bit of adult authority. A precocious child may feign sleep and read late into the night, clutching a cherished book (and a flashlight) under the covers, delighting in *Nancy Drew, Huck Finn,* or *The Hobbit.* He or she may prefer to be alone, may feel primed to move on and into the beckoning of an interior love.

Effective independence has a gigantic upside: Thinking skills get strengthened and refined as a child plans, initiates, and self-directs his or her play. The greater children's subjective safety, the sooner they'll explore their wider world. An entrepreneur reading these lines exclaimed,

"Yes, exactly! I couldn't wait to break free of limits, to leave home, to get out and test what I could do on my own." A typical high-school senior with whom I chatted repeated that refrain:

> My favorite time and place to be is late at night, home "alone" when the family's asleep and the house is all clean and there are no distractions. Then, finally I can think my own thoughts.

Such self-sufficient conduct easily perplexes adults. If parents or day-care supervisors assume a typical overseer's role, they could find, to their dismay, that the more they cling to their youngsters, the more they'll pull away. An emotionally healthy girl or boy rejects each hint of smothering or possessive control. Spiritually intelligent youngsters might even shy away from parents or close friendships. Not to worry: Early awakeners are not ax-murderers, and in a wholesome, happy household solitude rarely breeds antisocial tendencies. Quite the reverse.

Most religiously gifted children hanker for an occupied solitude. Their initial inspiration to lead a worshipful life often emerges as a sturdy self-authority. The inner actor longs for prayer, or wants time to contemplate, or gravitates to wise adults and other self-reliant children. Desires for engaged solitude direct the early choices.[17]

I'm convinced that all youngsters (indeed, all people) are potentially reflective giants who seek out growthful recreation in their own way if their call to wholeness is respected. Please note that early awakeners heed their inner call without external support. Without approval. Indeed, the force and charm of their own righteous ideas is sufficiently refreshing. It sustains. Let's give these youngsters some air. It sounds harsh, but as a wise professor of mine insisted, "We adults, parents included, should nurture, support, and discipline only as needed. Then step out of the child's light."

## Learning from Early Awakeners: Inspired Thought

Youngsters teach us that inspired thought is amplified as we:

- attend to the "activity" or presence of a holy (whole) idea within awareness,

- sense what activities contribute to joy and vital energy,

- take responsibility and initiative for learning.

Within some little children's hearts, a primordial knowing unfolds a saga of mythic proportion. Self-directed and authoritative, sooner than age four or five, inspired children sense who they are and who they are not. The live wires take stock of what's happening in and around them. From early age some seed of truth or right idea seems active in their awareness. They define their focus. They commit to lifelong endeavors. They may feel incredibly optimistic. Or not. They'll beat the odds of some difficulty. Or live with it as they must. They'll receive adulation in their area of talent. Or get rejected. Any and all of the above. It's consciousness, not circumstance, that sets early awakeners apart.

In the early 1900s Richard Bucke, M.D., investigated the evolution of higher awareness in adults. He identified several traits of an elevated mentality that he called "cosmic consciousness," for instance

- intellectual acuteness,
- moral elevation,
- all-embracing optimism,
- a sense of immortality and the indivisible, living nature of all things.

Bucke's subjects knew without learning from books, mentors, or school that "the universe is not a dead machine, but a living presence," that in its "essence and tendency it is infinitely good," and that individual life "is continuous beyond what is called death."[18] The individuals he studied — for example, Walt Whitman, Dante, Gautama the Buddha — assumed great initiative and responsibility for their learning. Such bare-bones proactivity exists in some young children, and we would do well to ask ourselves whether we are as diligent in the pursuit and application of meaningful knowledge as we could be. It does little good to initiate a day-trading enterprise if we're fascinated by antique trains. To be animated at the core through study and reflection, we'll need to affirm the quickening that leads us to unity, of the self we truly are.

# Chapter Two

# Animated Essence

*I am both brave and timid. And outgoing, too.*
— Student, age sixteen

Sometimes a parent's interests spark a child's essential, lifelong love. Writer Eudora Welty tells us that both of her parents could not give her enough books. Reading was the family's passion. They also bought her "toys that instruct": kites, trains, Erector sets. Especially the train symbolized her father's "fondest beliefs — in progress, in the future."[1]

Sometimes without assistance a child feels life tugging at the heart. G. K. Chesterton suggests that long before Francis of Assisi became a saint, he was listening for angels while listening for birds. As a boy, Albert Einstein sang " 'songs to God,' a sign of his chosenness... [and] Niels Bohr believed he was chosen to create a scientific renaissance in Denmark. Werner Heisenberg felt himself to be the scientific conscience of the German people."[2]

I frame early awakening within the broadest context of spiritual giftedness, defining "spiritual" as I have before: as that animating, intelligent, and loving essence pervading each one's ground of being.[3] There are thinking skills involved in heightened awareness — not just the caring-sharing, interpersonal cluster. Intuition, conceptualizing, and the resolving of paradox are only three of many capabilities enhanced by spiritual intelligence (see the chart on p. 13).

I focus "giftedness" through a spiritual lens. To me, all people are somehow gifted and endowed with inborn capacities. The word "gift" means a present, a legacy, an inheritance — a grace, if you will. Gifts are particular: If someone gives you theater tickets, the tickets don't give you entrée to every play in general, but to a specific production in a precise location on Broadway or in your home town.

Gifts also come with, or as, the package of each newborn child. Not everyone views giftedness in that way.[4] This should not derail us. As noted, my job here is not to debate the causes of giftedness. I'm not one to give ironclad advice on how to engineer worldly success or pump up children's ambition as if it were a flat tire. I'm laying bare my own realities and describing decades' worth of research and hands-on experience with the "such-ness" or vital element of the spiritually intelligent. I'm sharing my point of view: Critical, sagacious wellsprings prepare children for a lively, contributive life. I'm saying, let's not forget that animating influence. Let's bring that sweet fragrance, that unrepeatable life-force into each child's developmental mix. And our own.

## Overview: Animated Essence

An exquisite stirring or knowing ignites the child's initial fervor. The inspired youngster awakens to his or her inner world — commonly through books or, now, movies. There seems to be a progression here. A boy or girl senses a distinctive love within, feels the imagination as an inviting, readily available, and boundless resource. The child dips deep into the interior waters, gets a hunch, receives "directives," experiences a surge of energy, excitement, or vision of possibility, resulting in expression and relief. That's followed by more joyful curiosity, more beckoning — upon which the cycle repeats, intensifies, and potentially blesses the individual's entire life.

If that inspired progression is suppressed or endangered for whatever reason, this makes for apathy, dullness, repressed vitality. The still small voice is quelled. Deprived of opportunities to fulfill that seminal sequence, which to some extent depends on emotional safety, children can grow disoriented. We'll look at how severe trauma — called the "extreme situation" — so deftly strips away security that the integrity of life is at risk. Moreover, prolonged insecurity can abort or block healthy expressive drives and breed a learned helplessness and a belief in a punitive world. An education in fright can stymie intelligence of any sort.

Conversely, wholesome development encourages spiritual intelligence. Now children feel fated to contribute to others through their gifts. The animated essence produces feelings of being "anointed" or special, as though leading a charmed existence. Or they'll describe themselves as lucky. Bystanders sense they're in the company of one of life's ecstatic dancers.

Children growing whole feel something transcendent within. Perhaps it's a hidden theme of life, a nuance. For instance, young gifted scientists get focused very early. Their interests are stable "over many years."[5] That distinctive calling could make any child feel special.

Inspired children often understand that they are a conduit for transmitting the deepest truths of experience — much like Marcel Proust's idea that his writing was the sum of a *different* self than that which he expressed in social life or daily habits. Undeniably, such youngsters feel an idiosyncratic truth at their ground of being pressing for release.

That same sort of exuberance seems to have quickened the mind of the late statesperson Barbara Jordan, as she shaped a radiant leader's life. Compared to Jordan, lesser lights (perhaps equally talented and perhaps engaged in parallel efforts) lack her unbounded mind, her vision or hopeful self-confidence. Maybe that's why some leaders function not as statespersons but merely as "politicians."

## Devotional Inspirations

Precociously devoted individuals of varying faiths — Dietrich Bonhoeffer, Dorothy Day, Gandhi, Martin Luther King Jr. — are my prototypes for all this. So why don't all children sense their categorical imperatives from within? Because we groom them (and ourselves) away from the inner call. We teach girls and boys to be materially, not spiritually, successful. As Krishnamurti once noted, the standard education helps children blend into the crowd. What course of public school study asks anyone to cultivate spiritual self-realization? Only the rare teacher suggests that life is a sacred, integrative progression. Perhaps conveying that idea is not the job of educators, but surely it belongs to parents.

In the devout of every era and type, the inspired thoughts of the religiously gifted are conspicuous. They risk all to follow a high, ineffable dream. Artistic or "religiously gifted" youngsters can teach us much about animated essence. We should be studying them in our graduate courses of creativity. However, not all intuitive giants are religiously disposed. Therefore, I'm concentrating on creative children of every type. It is my conviction that spiritual intelligence is inborn — yes, God-given — and that a child's conduct often reveals the inner light. Many spiritually enlivened children share a disposition:

- they crave solitude and privacy for an adult-like, creative freedom;

- they seem to have an inspired "essence" or core being that is self-aware and distinctive;

- they are led by love, zeal, or continuity of interest.

For those who need a blueprint to understand inspiration, the religiously and artistically gifted reveal that quickened essence. They are highly receptive to their inner experience. They feel destiny's touch. They spot the sublime in the ordinary as did Catholic social activist Dorothy Day. Her instinct for contemplation was aroused in early childhood. As a girl, she prayed long and hard. She thought about issues of right and wrong. In his youth, Honoré de Balzac decided he'd be a writer. His mental processes were called "robust." Armed with "strong common sense" that guided his judgment, even as a boy he felt destined to accomplish "something great along that line, and composed at school, among other things, a treatise on the will and an epic poem."[6]

## A Transcendent Mind

I do not suggest religious or artistic experience is a child's only entry into spiritual insight. To the contrary. I see something luminous and sacred reflected by each one. Creation sparkles. Each life is a gift, and every talent, however supposedly mundane, casts a religious sheen over my sights. And people shine with light. Faith in the unseen good, simple decency, a discernible passion for some truth or reality beyond "self" — these traits characterize both the religiously gifted and early awakeners, secular though the latter may seem to some. Even unchurched youngsters preoccupied with what *we* label worldly pursuits reflect a transcendent mind. They, too, sense mystical forces, an inner voice. As Joseph Conrad said, " 'the inward voice' decides," and most youngsters directly feel what Albert Einstein termed cosmic religiosity. They may feel chosen for a particular way of life or endeavor or could experience reverence for the sanctity of their powers.[7] The sentiments of one "normal" sixteen-year-old I chatted with illustrate the point:

> I am imaginative and creative and hope to own a bike shop one day. My hobby is riding freestyle bikes. It takes a lot of creative skill to come up with new routines.
>
> To this point the three most positive influences on my inner life have been my hobby, God, and my parents. God is the creator, so he has full power over me in terms of influences. That's all I have to say.

We rarely credit artistic, athletic, musical, or scientific children with spiritual intelligence. It's as if we adults forget the seamless link between productive fervor of all kinds and a devotional, self-sacrificing knowing. That intimate understanding is so near and so dear to us that the Book of Proverbs instructs, "Say unto wisdom, Thou art my sister" (7:4).

## Led by Love

Our world's noblest contributors become global treasures precisely because their gifts express a useful intelligence that *is* love. From their ardors they enliven us. Great singers, dancers, athletes, or saints remind us of who we could be were we to break through our hard, dull shells of resistance. Perhaps only in our ultracompetitive, twenty-first-century culture must we remind ourselves that talent, virtue, and each shading of grace inject us with a bald craving for truth and wholesome growth. That is other-worldly bread. Certain infants are already ravenous, as one woman now in her seventies, recalls:

> My mother wrote in my Baby Book that, before I was three, I awoke in the middle of the night and caused my grandmother, with whom I slept, to get up and say my prayers with me — this, in a cold house. I have prayed steadily, from that day forth.

Longing can be transfiguring, can give us the power to move past earthly comforts and into our cold unknowns. Surrender to those unknowns is sacrificial and spiritually intelligent. Surrender animates us. It is motivating although, in the short run, such conduct may seem illogical.

## *Learning about Spiritual Intelligence: Animated Essence*

Early awakeners are only selectively consumed by their foundational ideas or projects. Not everything commands their attention. What does, they approach with single-minded devotion. Like other gifted creatives who have "a generalized sensitivity to problems," spiritually intelligent children discern when things are not right and know what needs doing.[8] From the inspired we learn to ask ourselves,

- What turns me on?
- What brings me to life?
- What sorts of traits, inclinations, and particularity make me "me"?

In her meticulously crafted biography of American miniaturist Eulabee Dix, JoAnn Ridley reinforces the notion of early, animated essence. In kindergarten Dix's artistic prowess was already obvious in a singular direction. By age eight, her teachers were making good use of those indigenous gifts for school projects. The child's aesthetic temperament was also fine-tuned. When Eulabee and her little friends cut out paper dolls, the young artist

> had no patience with the careless ones who left white space around the cut-outs. But she was fascinated by her mother's ability to cut silhouettes and would sit quietly while [the figures] emerged from scissors and letter paper.... Today, a number of her own silhouettes are in private and museum collections.[9]

Strong drive, a disposition to achieve something rare, a lifelong interest spurred by a whole ideal that was

cherished in mind, and stubborn optimism seem to have
nurtured Dix's entire existence. She was the sort who,
even when financially strapped, displayed style — an op-
ulent, sophisticated chic. From girlhood through old age
she possessed flair, fortitude, a sense of emotional safety.
Economic, social, and family circumstances offered Dix
countless chances to fail, to give up. She never took
advantage of these. That's spiritually intelligent.

# Chapter Three

# Intuitive Authority

*I'm bright, solitary, and complicated. I'm skeptical and pessimistic.*                    —Student, age fifteen

Once upon a time in South Chicago, a child and her eight siblings lived in an ethnic neighborhood with their grandparents. The elderly couple seldom spoke to the youngsters and fed them lore about a very strict god. Now an adult, the individual recollects, "Our world was filled with the devil and the evil eye." She had to be ever vigilant. The nuns in her religion class warned the students not to spend too much time bathing. It would lead to "an occasion of sin." This notion terrified the girl, who could not figure out how much time in the tub was safe:

> Then I heard about a girl who was so good that when she sat in church to pray, she would actually float above the pew. I desperately wanted to be holy enough to float too. I asked my very friendly guardian angel...to help me be very good, but we were unsuccessful.
>
> Girls had their ears pierced to let the evil spirits out of their heads (so that they wouldn't get headaches). Once my grandfather became ill, so we

rented a leech from the local barber to get the bad
blood out. Grandpa died anyway.

Longing for holiness, that child must have clung to a
private hope of better days. That cleaving is a sign that
love is alive and present. If, for example, you'd ask me
how youngsters brought up with so great an awareness
of gloom can develop good humor or hope, I'd answer
this way: Whenever children sense love at their ground
of being, they feel uplifted. Beyond a grim household,
over and above false notions of sin or guilt, they'll be
mysteriously comforted, even optimistic about their future. Love arranges the child's understanding of life. And
could we agree that the experiencing of love at one's
ground of being is somehow unmerited? It is a grace. In
other words, I don't know "why" one child feels love
and another doesn't or why one is divinely protected
and another isn't. No amount of force, no trendy child-
rearing method, no unholy lie — however seductive —
evokes or suppresses love's power. Love's impersonal (or,
if you prefer, "nonpersonal") warmth comforts a boy or
girl through trouble or conflict.[1] Love stirs compassion
and prepares the heart to forgive. Even a little child can
gaze with radical simplicity on life's stark radiance. That
deeper sight is inspired — animating, vivifying, stirring,
quickening — and it relates to wisdom. And it triggers
the need to consecrate life.


### Overview: Intuitive Authority

Early awakeners, guided by wisdom, transfer a concrete
organizing power from vibrant inner realities to their

external purposes. Their gifts are less obscured by, say, some trouble than are other children's. Somewhere in consciousness the liar that accuses most of us is subdued. Inspired thought releases a universal love from which all acts of compassion, service, and forgiveness flow. What's possible or desirable becomes visible in and through the child's thinking.

Love's organizing power is the ability to move self and world toward the apprehended good. Children who sense that universal love tend to possess not only authority but also inner order, defined by educator Grace Pilon as "a feeling of well-being in the mind." It is as if some youngsters think and then choose the good or possible into existence. That's inspired. It's also the stuff of which true authority is born.

## Intuitive Authority as a Spiritual Prod

That ordering love is somehow validating, and it has global elements. Universal love is potentially available to each child. A case in point: As a boy César Chávez seems to have been attuned to what needed doing. The Chávez family had fled an ordeal of poverty in Mexico for the American Dream in Arizona, where they created a viable freight business and a homestead. Chávez recalled a happy boyhood. His grandmother's religious teachings influenced him positively. Unfortunately, when he entered public school, Chávez met with corporal punishment for speaking Spanish. He was humiliated for mispronouncing English words and labeled a "dirty Mexican" by the Anglo children. When fights broke out over the name-calling, the Anglo students were protected by teachers.

Then, too, economic hardships engulfed the Chávez family. They lost their homestead to back taxes and were forced into migrant farm work.[2] Thus, long before adulthood, César Chávez felt the agony of financial insecurity, backbreaking manual labor, and racial injustice. Those circumstances must have planted the seeds for his political activism. Surely some internal representation of love — fairness, justice, equal treatment for all — inspired César's later commitment to better the lot of migrant workers. I see that animation as a goad of spiritual intelligence, a goad accompanied by a big-picture view of life's demands and the commitment to meet those.

To progress wholesomely, each child needs (and actively searches for) upliftment. Each wants spiritual prototypes. In his grandmother, Chávez found one inspiring heroine. His family also seems to have been cohesive, their effect enduring. I can almost hear their dinner-time talks about human rights or fair play. Other spiritual models must have surfaced from ancestral myths and the links of daily life. That positive mentoring spirit exists in almost anything that provides children with the vision they need to move beyond discord and transform it into something whole and useful. Even nominal support from a dysfunctional family enhances the likelihood that girls and boys will tap into loving, productive values. If children are disciplined fairly, their self-controls develop. That, too, enables them to tackle challenges. By contrast, no matter how privileged children are, if an adult — or the environment — devastates their inner life too early, if they're lacking in elemental love, they may feel trapped, even bitter, as did one fifteen-year-old, who, after our talk, sent me an unsigned note saying,

To this point no positive influences have touched my life because my parents don't care about me. And I don't care about other people, either.

Why is it then that severe distress mysteriously helps some youngsters? Or that torment, instead of being a permanent wound (from which the ineffectual never recover), becomes stigmata of sorts — a necessary wounding and precursor for the mental clarity that continuously prods a renewal in truth? One answer is that youngsters can and do reinterpret their pain.

### Spiritual Intelligence and the Creative Process

Early awakeners, like adults who endure, manage to derive their place in the scheme of things from the sorts of hardships that undermine others.[3] They ride trauma as a chariot of growth, transmuting despair into joy. That tough-minded response serves their future, and it's not unusual. One of the articulate fifteen-year-old students I spoke with described what that alchemy entailed for her:

My mother's death strengthened me. Strangely, that has been, thus far, the most productive influence on my inner life. Her dying forced me to find myself, to really dig deep, to sort out what's important.

By making something whole out of something broken, that teenager moved beyond a heartrending event. To "dig deep, to sort out what's important" stimulated her recuperative energy. Digging deep and sorting out are emotionally organizing acts that support an inner authority. Surveying one's inner landscape, protecting its truths, is what it means to have dominion over one's experience.

Challenged on a profound emotional level, some children cope. They build skill. They hold an idea that says, "I'm the sort of kid who will figure out what to do." That's an illogical process. It moves from inner to outer. Starts and stops. Confounds us for a time. One poet found an ironic but comforting logic in this. Blocked in one area of life, he consciously freed up another, more satisfying area, thereby solving his problem and unleashing his creativity: "As a boy I could not speak of my pain, so I wrote poetry instead. Words and images led me to a greater life — over and above the pain."

A sense of a "greater life, over and above the pain" ignites some children's core ambitions, inspiring an ordering idea. That is inspiration's marker. The spiritually intelligent may "see" their greater life as a vision. Artist Georgia O'Keeffe said she felt — or saw — geometric shapes and forms in her mind that demanded expression. Others feel their greater life when meeting or reading about a hero, or they'll "hear" a summons: More harmonious conditions await. Above all, when love is present, an idea of promise knocks at the door of the youngster's awareness. That hopeful knock is ordering. It asks a child, asks anyone, to *claim* life, to possess it, to master or "own" time, the results wanted, the creative methods used. What else is an ordering idea but an intelligible imperative, a conception, plan, or understanding of what's already whole and unrestrained? Secret aims, born of one ordering idea that's focused early, have the power to shape an entire life.

An idea houses its own power and its design. An idea is a force.[4] Its seed is in itself. The germ of any right idea precedes inspired solutions. It insists we look to what's possible and overlook mere earthly constraints. That's intuitive authority.

Several factors further these authoritative, organizing processes:

- the call of some preexisting truth;
- controlled fervor and a developing point of view;
- constancy of interest or vocational leadings.

You've probably sensed your own preexisting truth, your "right ideas." Weren't there irritants in your youthful surroundings that made you vow to change things, someday, as soon as feasible? Didn't you want to express more beauty, peace, or kindness in your life? Or discover certain laws in math or sailing? Did a teacher belittle you in front of friends, causing your determination never to be cruel to anyone? Might your current interest in coaching, teaching, or graphics have started back then? Were you entranced with business? Or making and investing money? Or did you simply want to grow up to be a decent human being? Your answers will show you how love has guided your life.

Similarly, the inspired child grows by *intending* to forge a character, career, or friendships just so, just as visioned at best. One child-development specialist proposes that some achievement-challenges "never disappear." True, ageism, sexism, poverty, and perhaps especially racism are hurdles that not everyone can scale. Nevertheless, the thirty-nine high-achieving women interviewed by Dorothy Ehrhart-Morrison credit the variables of inner strength for their success. As one woman explained,

My desire to achieve and the positive feelings I have about myself helped me overcome all barriers that researchers say are responsible for failure in the underclass.[5]

Early awakeners don't just dream. They are precocious, effective activists. Sooner rather than later, they set out to achieve their dreams, as two more illustrations reveal.

Rejected by schoolmates and neighbors when he was first diagnosed with the AIDS virus, Ryan White was forced to relocate with his family to another, friendlier town. After the move and until his death White appeared to live under an umbrella of grace. Who could have imagined that what started as a thorny path would have led to international stature, transforming White into an All-American hero? I only speculate that Ryan White's self-respect was whole — a veritable subjective hologram. That right idea — self-respect, his sense that "it's how you live your life that counts" — helped him transcend anguish, drew him to the rightness of a specific vocation, in his case a leader's life. From about age thirteen to age sixteen (when he died) White used his trial as would any gifted leader, as a vehicle to communicate his vision, his values, his educator's message: "It's how you live your life that counts."[6] White leaned on his inborn charisma and on other relational and teaching talents to inform and elevate the collective mind about AIDS. He had authority enough to touch the hearts of schoolchildren, the media, and citizens the world over. Within that young lad's challenge lived a *victory* that "never disappears."

I see such rare children as secular saints. They're "normal" youngsters with one foot planted in mundane realms and the other in a holistic transcendence. Early awakeners bridge the gap between what some consider the virtuous excesses of religious saints (to whose sufferings or renunciations few relate) and our own efforts to be kind, well-integrated persons.[7]

Consider Barbara Jordan, another national treasure. She grew up in Houston's Fifth Ward, called the largest ghetto in all of Texas. She was the youngest of three girls, and her family lived in confined quarters. For years Jordan and her sisters shared a single bed. Jordan's parents were of modest means but active, civic-minded members of their community and church leaders. Ambitious, tenacious, and eager to prove herself, Jordan was "seized" by an inspired idea — to practice law — after she heard lawyer Edith Sampson speak about careers at school.[8] Barbara's self-respect and sense of purpose appear to have been high. These traits sponsor credibility. One imagines that, like Ryan White and César Chávez, she met discrimination, facing the prejudices of her era and locale with dignity and courage. How was that possible without a symmetry or interior authority guiding her young life?

Jordan had witnessed her maternal grandfather, a cafe owner, unjustly convicted of assault with intent to commit murder. He had accidentally shot a white policeman while chasing a thief from his cafe. Jordan's grandfather, "along with many other wrongly convicted blacks in Texas," was eventually pardoned by Governor Miriam Ferguson.[9] The episode may have reinforced Jordan's instinctive call to champion equal treatment for all people under the law. It's clear that she knew she lacked the cosmetic arsenal that some women dip into when battling to get ahead. It's also certain that she interpreted her circumstances positively. Barbara Jordan kept a big, wide-open view of her potential. Intent on making a positive contribution, Jordan scoured the biographies of successful people. She bolstered the well-defined work ethic and certitude that her parents had stressed: If she applied herself, she could be almost anything. Apply herself she did.

## Controlled Fervor and a Point of View

We learn from Barbara Jordan's example that enduring inspiration involves an elemental passion, but of a managed sort. Jordan possessed *controlled* fervor: That's tactical patience in the sense that Eugene Herrigel may have meant when he wrote that to gain an enlightened mastery through archery the effective wait intelligently: They let go of "self," leaving cares and ambitions behind "so decisively that nothing more is left . . . but purposeless tension."[10] That same managed passion could be framed in Father William McNamara's terms: Ardor can prompt our participation in the boundless life of God's spirit, with its "infinitely wild" quality and its incarnation of the governing passion. Somehow, says McNamara, that prompting from within fuses all our little wants into one overriding, single-minded aim.[11] No one has the density of character or "is-ness" of that true authority without inward control. Passion alone gives us energy, drive — perhaps mania. Controlled ardor impresses the mind with the skill and patience needed to run the race set before us and actualize our life's vision.

Am I alone in spotting in some young children a spontaneous desire to fuse with some superordinate, single-minded aim? Desire like that organizes us. It is a power that both produces and delivers the goods. Controlled passion sets goals. It cultivates other self-disciplines, like perseverance. Children like Chávez, White, and Jordan pace themselves. They arrest their impulsivity and learn to wait. They bide their time. Even in childhood, Arasteh's lexicon of "final integration" applies: The inner world of certain youngsters steers them toward oneness with whatever they desire, be it community leadership or comprehending the structure of a molecule. Controlled, patient fervor also paves the way for the twice-born experience: the rebirth that unfolds unitive consciousness.

Certain young people feel as if they're pursuing a lost love with whom they must unite. Their tracking impulse sets up a trajectory from which tenacity, wise choices, and an enduring point of view arise. What we call a vision or "dream" is in fact a seed of wholeness. For individuals like Barbara Jordan, Ryan White, or César Chávez who persist, that self-revealing seed eventually sprouts into a plausible manifestation of truth.

## Intensity and Constancy

Two more factors mark the life of the creative and spiritually authoritative adults: intensity and constancy of gifts.[12] We note in children, too, that these qualities transform mere musical, mathematical, kinesthetic, or inventive prowess into a transfiguring, comprehensible joy. When first meeting their universe of gifts — say, numbers, sound, or movement — such children may feel as if they're "coming home." It is not togetherness, teamwork, or emotional intelligence that counts for so much in the spiritually bright, but an internal coherency that organizes and shapes the life they intend to have. People like a César Chávez or a Barbara Jordan will use complex leadership skills to enter their universe of wholeness, while a Ryan White enlists a mix of teaching and communication talents to express his vision, and a Eulabee Dix adopts art as her transformational vehicle.

## Comforting Companions

In the company of such children our window on the world opens. Our horizons widen. Our optimism is renewed. Even in youth, the spiritually intelligent can be comforting "companions." They're at once universal and individuated — peerless. Despite idiosyncrasies, they reveal some glad trace of ourselves. If we see ourselves in them, an intriguing transference may occur. For example, every Olympic competition is populated with young athletes with whom we identify and on whom we project our own tenacity or latent grace. Similarly, young winners of good citizenship or spelling bee awards arouse our pride and self-worthy instincts. As we cheer them on we're also rooting for ourselves to try harder, to win. In part, our projections mean we've externalized, or cast onto another, something of ourselves. The Sufi mystic-poet Rumi framed his projection of spiritual love with lines penned to his beloved human mentor, Shams of Tabriz:

> We were anxious once before,
> Now in your image we are warmly comforted.[13]

As the calming image of Shams of Tabriz coaxed out Rumi's preexisting harmony, so do children who represent beauty or virtue to us coax out our hope. Or hostility.

Depending on our background, exemplary youngsters can provoke erotic love, jealousy, or bitterness. This phenomenon is subtle, so often masked in childhood. Adults commonly deny feeling envy or animosity toward anyone, but especially a child. We understand such emotions by virtue of our own experience, as adults. An adult Barbara Jordan realized that she struck some people the wrong way — as odd or out of place.[14] I don't know when her sense of being reviled or feared began — perhaps in her youth. By means of her superior intelligence and eloquence, Jordan overcame such insults. She came to embody a universal justice and vigorous power. She manifested fairness to the downtrodden and the privileged alike.[15] In her last years, wheelchair-bound and suffering from multiple sclerosis and leukemia, Jordan accepted her oceanic charisma:

> She understood that she was black and she was more than black . . . that when Barbara Jordan spoke, America listened. It was important to her that black America listened, but she clearly was a woman who had and knew she had influence beyond her own racial group. . . . She was a very thoughtful politician, but she was [simultaneously] a woman who believed in the Constitution because she was going to make it be right. This was not blind faith. This was the sense that if you struggle, if you insist, if you are determined, you can [bring your ideals to life].[16]

Through our identifications with extraordinary youngsters — and our transferences — *we* change. At best, the child draws out from us something we'd forgotten: poise, strength, enhanced eloquence. Anyone who's ever felt soothed by talking with a trusted friend knows what that's like. Even a brief encounter with, say, a beloved teacher or a healer can confer that same sort of renewal. This issue has a downside and, partly, explains the discomfort, the anger, or jealousy churned up in some parents by their own children. When elders apprehend a purity or luster in the youngster (some shine or opportunity the adults fear they'll never possess), toxic regret or hostility toward the child may emerge. With that comes an unhealthy attachment. I believe that much child neglect, abuse, both overcontrol and overprotection take root in the unhealthy bond that, left unchecked, can undermine spiritual intelligence.

## Vocational Leadings

Early awakeners find their vocation (or life's work) by employing their most intimate experiences, both joyful and despairing. A vocation leads us to ourselves distinctively, yet within the context of life in community. Spiritually intelligent children cultivate their gifts. An interior logic or coherency enters into their mundane choices. Of course, for a true vocation to emerge, the child's ambitions, talents, and subjective energy must propel the choices (not the parents'). Furthermore, I refer here to youngsters' self-initiated and fulfilling engagements, not to their achievements per se. Competitive, domineering parents so easily contaminate vocational leanings. For instance, some adults are starved for the reflected glory (or revenue) to be derived from their offspring's accomplishments. They press their youngster into bogus, unfulfilling arenas. We witness various degrees of that malady at Little

League games when parents rant at children's so-called ineptness or losses.

## Learning from Early Awakeners: Intuitive Authority

A vocation and perhaps primordial, archetypal drives exist when children feel, as did one young rock climber, "There's just something about this activity that's really me." Much youthful exploration is zestful and reliably foreshadows a fulfilling destiny, as is examined more closely in chapter 5. With an authentic interest comes a sense of play or liberty. When that deeply organizing love and labor marry, the offspring is fun, as J. Krishnamurti explained so well:

> Real life is doing something which you love to do with your whole being so that there is no inner con- tradiction, no war between what you are doing and what you think you should do.[17]

Robert Rodriguez, a young filmmaker, was hailed na- tionally for producing *El Mariachi* (and for self-funding the movie for $7,000). Talent unleashed and orchestrated Rodriguez's love of filmmaking. As he tells it, he simply fell in love with making movies: "When I was 11, my dad brought home a VCR and a camcorder. I've been making videos with my nine brothers and sister since."[18] Stephen Spielberg's youthful zest for filmmaking ap- pears to mirror this sort of pattern: His father gave him a camera and the rest is history. Few children act out this concentrated dynamic on a grand scale. Most spiritually intelligent girls and boys are simply preparing themselves for adulthood. Even so, by looking carefully we see a progressive, leaderlike coherency in every authentic engagement. As long as the adults in charge don't devalue or corrupt children's psychic world, youngsters can "fall in love" with their own delights. The encounter heals, directs, and organizes life. It provides authority. A favorite activity reconciles opposites and fleshes out aspects of the unknown. We adults may interrupt the incubation period of whatever turns on our children's creative juices by looking to capable young people as our confidants, contemporaries, or, worse, as caretakers. To repeat my professor's helpful precept, stewardly adults "lend support, provide resources, and then step out of their child's light." Alas, parents and teachers too often lean on effective children as family or classroom leaders. Typically, that robs youngsters of their own delights. This is natural, often builds the child's capabilities, and happens routinely with an only or oldest child. But it also redirects talent and may disorganize a youngster emotionally.

Consider an insecure, unstable, or infantile parent who regards a capable, attractive youngster jealously, as a competitor. Anything along these lines undermines the child's best interests. Early awakeners teach us that it's important to guard and encourage our own vivid interests, to let our thinking and choices proceed from our inherent gifts and the creative process linked to our spiritual realities. So comes *our* freedom, our inner order, our zest.

The spiritually intelligent also show us how to employ our pain in the service of our lives. We, like all such children

- can find blessed lessons in an ordeal,
- can rise above suffering, using it to grow,
- can use joy and despair alike to locate a vocation — a transcendent reason for being.

Truthful unfolding seems the fait accompli of the spiritually intelligent. It proceeds no matter what else seems to be going on. Integrity, or wholeness, directs all our little subselves and conflicting pulls into a force that enfleshes a purpose larger than we are. Rather than resulting in chaos, that integrity reveals what spiritual directors and psychologists call "is-ness": a character structure and a present-centeredness that orders existence. Therefore integrity is also an ongoing guide, a movement, or a *becoming* to which we instinctively reach out, after some peak joy or trauma shakes us up. As we grow whole, the Army's motto, "Be all you can be," is usually what we have in mind.

If children can hear and heed their "still, small voice," surely we adults can too. We can make choices in the direction of our interior authority, the Spirit within that awaits to

- arrange our understanding of life,
- animate and vivify our conscious choices,
- transfer organizing power from interior realities to our exterior purposes.

Our job, whatever our age, is to discipline our fervor, to control our passion. With skill and singleminded intent we thereby surrender to the spiritual authority that orders our unfolding.

## Personal Patterns

I know something about the importance of singleminded intent and the need for it. I know about intuitive authority and befriending chaos and have watched early trauma subvert the inspired thought of someone I loved. My childhood was hardly serene.[19] Not until adulthood did I realize the severity of my own anguish which — given the repeated onslaughts of demoralizing events — amounted to a shell-shock of sorts. This despite the fact that my parents were bright, wholly original people — extraordinarily kind and morally elevated, not merely cultured. I idealized them both.

Around my fourth year, my parents got caught up in a series of trials. Their vale of tears undid them. To be accurate, family life was never a steady downpour of gloom. Nevertheless, there were chaotic storms. My father spent years as a prisoner of war in a Japanese "internment" center. My mother had a debilitating mental illness. My half-brother was sent away to boarding school. There were significant financial reverses, around which time my father died, prematurely. Subsequently, our little family just dissolved.

Life on the edge became my teacher — austere, unremitting, yet weirdly liberating and organizing nonetheless. I suffocated under the weight of my mother's increasing emotional dependence. Observing what I considered her futile strategies to be an effectual free spirit, I determined that "the good life" demanded lucidity, creative competence, and the ability to function ably as one's norm. Admittedly, I functioned — indeed, I survived — by pressing forward. Love guarded me, and "His hands maketh

whole" (Job 5:18). On some level, I was guided from
within. My conscious maneuver to leave home, my refusal to be a malleable daughter and a conventional wife
or mother forms an arc of choices that fulfills not only my
own but also my parents' deepest aspirations. The ones
they never quite achieved.

## *In Sum*

Images of what could be, whispers of good things to come,
feelings of promise — all these are wisdom's germ of truth,
the divinity at our ground of being that heals our broken-
ness, promotes a sense of order, and a vision of what needs
doing or is important. As Isaiah promises, so does a little
one become a thousand and preach good tidings unto the
meek and brokenhearted, and proclaim liberty unto the
captives (Isa. 60:22; 61:1). In my eyes, that becoming, that
preaching, that proclaiming is born of intuitive authority.

# Chapter Four

# Heeding Love

*I'd say I'm cheerful, artistic, considerate, silly, and
a ham.* — Student, age fifteen

Writer James Baldwin's stepfather was a preacher and a
laborer. Reverend Baldwin was an unsuccessful father to
young James. He appears to have been threatened by the
boy's gifts. He ridiculed James. Called him ugly. Subjected
his stepson to physical abuse: beatings for trivial mistakes; a circumcision long after infancy. He tried to thwart
James's reaching out to books, movies, and mentors that
might open a window on a wide world — the one that
repeatedly rejected the insecure and failing Reverend.[1]

When his stepfather advised James, around his four-
teenth birthday, to quit school and get a job, biographer
David Leeming reports that the boy demonstrated resolve.
He would have none of that. Young James walked in
truth. Insisted on continuing with his education. Turned
to other adults for support. Given his prodigious writing,
teaching, preaching, and conceptual gifts, James summoned up the courage to reject the narrow, lackluster
life his stepfather had in mind for him. On the coun-
sel of his friend Countee Cullen, James applied to and
was enrolled in the De Witt Clinton High School in the
Bronx, whose famous graduates include Richard Avedon,

George Cukor, Douglas Fairbanks, Sr., Burt Lancaster, Neil Simon, and Richard Hofstader.[2] James Baldwin heeded love. Vibrantly inspired youngsters like James tend to know what they need. Not always. If adults or other influences are too dominant, despite the talent pressing at the child, a charge of love can be ignored. In which case, it percolates underground.

## Overview: Heeding Love

No one heeds love who substitutes rigid, overobedient, or overcontrolled responses for learning, or who can't or won't let go of a parent, having a parent nearby, or being smothered.[3] We have seen that healthy growth asks children to embrace some degree of insecurity. Adults advance this task by setting up an atmosphere in which youngsters can explore their unknowns, thus inching into a world beyond easy answers, away from mothers, fathers, and conventional approval or beliefs. A radical knowing, intuitive in the main, spurs those steps. The early work to heed love is varied. It is as multifaceted as we are. Heeding love is *the* critical task of spiritual growth; therefore each chapter in this book returns to it.

Even a brief glance at the James Baldwin anecdote tells us that girls and boys who protect their interests, time, privacy, commitments, and the authenticity of their relationships can stay faithful to genuine experience. This could explain why some adolescents spend so many hours holed up in their rooms. There, they're alone. In private, they ponder what it means to grow up. They must separate emotionally from their parents or other authority figures (an altogether healthy task). In solitude they begin to disentangle themselves from false gods, hurtful friends, even a parent's seemingly reasonable wishes. Be assured, that work only *begins* in youth. For most, heeding love is a lifetime's occupation. In this, clarity seems synonymous with inspired thought.

We parents, teachers, and researchers must feel our way into the experience of youngsters like James Baldwin. We need empathy to understand how they feel, what they require by way of support or resources to develop successfully despite the vagaries of new experience or whatever obstructs their way. Their surefootedness, their knack of "rising to the occasion," like ours, involves grace and intuition. All this becomes possible by heeding love — the early "work."

## Personal Patterns

My childhood's heeding of love asked me to harmonize many discordancies, like the tug-of-war between my spiritual drives and more cowardly forces that tried to appease — and please — my parents. Both my mother and father were sophisticated. Any dogma seemed too restrictive to house the mind and style in which they lived. Herewith an initial rupture: I thought about God a lot. In particular, when it came to me and God, my dad consciously, philosophically, tried to restrain his charismatic influence. As a preschooler testing her father, I once asked him point-blank whether he believed in God. He answered that because parents too easily sway their young in any direction it was *my* job to fathom my own heart. Satisfied, I gladly took on the grandeur of that task.

Then too, I was instantly affected by the subjective

vibration of those around me — especially, my mother. When she was distraught and hovering too closely, I felt dread, then irritation, then impending doom. Just because you're young doesn't mean you don't sense invasion. Yet I could never quite articulate my feelings of ominous encroachment. The longer I held my tongue — concealed my feelings — the more hammered and fearful I felt. "Honor thy father and mother" I had read and dutifully believed that meant, "Don't speak your truths." Polite I was taught to be. Polite I was. And for a long time said nothing. Or, more accurately, nary a peep that had effect. In dread, I just distanced myself from my mother's disorganizing undertow. Not that the rest of the family didn't find her agitating, but I alone recoiled. How could that be? Years passed without answer.

Finally in adulthood I happened on two clues. One relates to what's now known as posttraumatic stress syndrome.[4] As each episode of my mother's illness intensified, each new cycle was more menacing to me. Over time, a fragrance, a tone of voice, a season vividly brought back the distressing experience. Back then no one knew that withdrawal was integral to healing.

The second clue involved the withdrawal motifs that typify the *norm* of some creative children, those with heightened sensitivities. The irony is that I sense both my mother and I share an acute awareness. We simply reacted differently when the pressure was on. For whatever reason, she could not function appropriately.

Sensitive means "receptive, alive to, impressionable." Acutely receptive youngsters have a built-in radar for all sorts of stimuli. They shrink from certain disquieting relationships as an inherent coping mechanism. Those of us with artistic, creative, or spiritual gifts may be lightning rods for the profound emotional aftershocks of early trauma. Fortunately, our creative work, a vocation of any sort, restores presence of mind. In retrospect, it seems that while I was defending my stability by backing away from my mother, she was no doubt shielding her own emotions by setting things up to avoid overstimulation with an energetic child, a spouse, or who knows what else. That, too, is heeding love. Its inspirations ask us to maintain our equilibrium as a precursor to gaining a more reliable compassion.

### Structure vs. Stimulation

A study of some ninety gifted boys and girls ranging from four to twenty-two years of age (with IQ scores from 130 to 200) determined that they shared several related traits. Two of these — excitability and sensitivity — seem germane. Excitability is related to sensitivity. It involves a

> high energy level, emotional reactivity and high arousal of the central nervous system, [with] all three aspects of the trait not necessarily present in one person.[5]

Naturally, each child responds idiosyncratically to the stimulus of play and people. Each requires differing amounts of self-initiated novelty and varying degrees of orderly, structured experience.

Neurologist Oliver Sacks, who carved a healer's vocation out of a hellish childhood during World War II, has aptly noted that "we all have to make our own worlds. Our worlds are totally embodied in our brains. And if we lose one world, yet another world may emerge."[6]

Indeed, some researchers believe that our nervous systems appear to be the basis for what we call "intellect."[7] The spiritually intelligent

- are acutely *aware* of their interior universe,

- are easily *identified* with experience,

- *feel* so in accord with experience that both the ecstasy of oneness and the sometimes intemperate withdrawal reflex are spontaneous.

More study is warranted about how specific types of spiritual or inventive intelligences demand specific stimulus barriers. I suspect that the use of certain drugs, nicotine, caffeine, and alcohol is an attempt to block a steep climb of arousal — both the pleasurable and the discordant, negative sort — while temporarily boosting vital energy. Solitude, stillness, prayer, or, say, yoga and meditation techniques, contemplation of every sort (e.g., on music, nature, poetry, and sacred literature) offer healthier routes to the same ends.

Author John Briggs suggests that the creatively gifted use their empathy and intensified sensitivity to absorb the whole world. He tells us that poet John Keats believed people of genius are so keenly receptive "to sorrow, joy, the commonplace, the heroic" that their peaks of openness spark intimacy with all existence.[8] Experientially they unite with others. As Keats tells it, "If a sparrow comes before my Window I take part in its existence and pick about the Gravel."[9]

Pianist Lorin Holander admitted that at three years old he merged with the very notes he played. Holander did not merely pound the ivories as might other infants, but consciously chose each key. He knew that when he played a note he would achieve union with that note.[10] That anticipation of oneness reinforces the idea of spiritual intelligence previously presented: The inspired child seeks unity with an interior love, feeling a degree of such intense absorption it could prove overwhelming. Thus the need to withdraw self-protectively from excess stimulation. Relationships or activities that seem mildly invigorating to most adults prove extremely unsettling to some children. Those whose minds lift into an easy transcendence may need added protection in the form of structure, stabilizing routines, and reliable, grounded supervisors. I believe this need continues in adulthood.

Years ago, as a student-teacher, I learned the Windy-Day Rule: Help girls and boys manage their inner tempests — the feelings aroused by wild wind gusts and even wilder recess play. On windy days, little children mimic the weather, resonating with it. They run around the playground in a frenzy, often screaming at the top of their lungs as they fly about. Uncontrolled excitement increases anxiety. That same agitation blocks learning. Experienced teachers insist students take a five-minute, "heads-down" rest after recess. They report few discipline problems. Those who forget such sensible protocols (or who are themselves disquieted) lose their class's attention. Ordering tasks or a short rest after recess or listening to a story or soothing music and of course the influence of steadying teachers all help children regain self-control.

For young children, even the normal course of events warrants shelter from adult chaos.

## Self-Sheltering in Childhood

Time has taught me that a child's recoil from anyone (or anything) is simply *data:* an intelligible language about some aspect of inner ordering. Adults can and must learn to decipher these behavioral cues. Both the fight response and the flight response are worthy self-sheltering devices. Gavin De Becker, an expert on predicting violent behavior, contends that the word "no" is a complete sentence, yet — especially when uttered by children or women — it is too easily discounted or ignored.

Most adolescents are shrewd judges of character whose withdrawal from an adult is often critical to self-sheltering. They'll instantaneously "read" an aunt, a teacher, or a coach — gravitate toward, shy away from, or even ridicule a grown-up in an eyewink. Their response reveals their humor, their tastes, their sense of propriety. Who knows how many abused children could be protected if the adults around them trusted the youngster's spontaneous wisdom to stay with or exit a relationship. Both recoil and attractions flow from "heeding love."

Keen sensitivity during a brief girlhood incident caused Dorothy Day to reflect on religious matters throughout the balance of her life. Day bounded into a friend's home in search of her playmate. She came upon a neighbor, Mrs. Barrett, on her knees praying. Day empathized. She felt a "burst of love" for Mrs. Barrett, feelings that ignited her own desire to pray. From then on, Day knelt in prayer daily until her own knees ached, and daily prayer led Day to an active, strenuous faith.[11]

A young poet's withdrawal from playmates or parents could enhance his inborn gifts. For Georgia O'Keeffe, "solitary hours nurtured her imagination [and] also strengthened her natural inclination to have things her own way."[12] Even adults who are wide open to experience, inspired — aware of whatever's going on around them — are susceptible to stresses of all sorts.[13] Understanding this aspect of spiritual intelligence in children helps us understand ourselves.

Regarding any youngster's flight from parents or teachers, other factors come into play. Repeatedly we hear that children act out an adult's unspoken wishes. They mirror what they perceive the adults value. Some preschoolers weep violently when parents drop them off at classroom doors. Perhaps these toddlers accurately discern their parents' separation anxieties. They sense that the adults dread not the parting but reunion at day's end. Tiny children are alert enough inwardly to uncover their parents' or teachers' deepest secrets. Parents who push children away may have clingy offspring. When adults cling, it is the child who often recoils. Such are the ways of wisdom.

## Wholesome Independence

Being able to separate from our parents is a basic skill. We don't hear much about that. In so-called primitive cultures, ritualized puberty rites transform adolescents' loyalties from dependency to healthy autonomy. Those societies recognize that only independent, contributive individuals sustain the well-being of a community. Today's so-called progressive cultures frequently lack a vernacular, time frames, and passageways for youth to transition to healthy autonomy. Little wonder then that so many social institutions — schools included — now groan under the weight of the dysfunctional, like the aggressively needy.

Diaries of pioneers who journeyed West in covered wagons tell a different tale: Separation rituals were sewn into the very fabric of daily affairs. Youngsters traveled through blistering heat and freezing cold, often on foot. Despite that, they functioned. They fed and cared for mules, oxen, and horses. They supervised younger children. They labored physically at strenuous chores, didn't take breaks, and were severely punished if they slacked off. Normal routines hardened the young, were a survival necessity, and acclimated girls and boys for premature, weighty responsibilities. Children who lost their mothers and fathers to illness and death had to fend for themselves, as if they were adults. Adolescents married at fourteen or earlier, had babies at fifteen, and frequently wore out at thirty. Childhood deaths were common.[14]

Twenty-first-century children are new pioneers. They may feel ill-equipped for their life's journey despite society's overall improvements in physical comforts, hygiene, sanitation, personal freedoms, or education and technology. As I write these words, I hear reports about adults in their twenties and thirties who return to live at their parents' home without embarrassment after commonplace mishaps: When they realize their incomes are insufficient to support their preferred lifestyles; when they're blue after a divorce; when they're suffering from fatigue or need a reliable babysitter for their young. Some parents

now shore up children long past their college graduation, through job searches and beyond. So complex is
modern life that today more than a million grandparents
are raising their children's children. The basic skills of
hearty independence need reinstatement. We shall revisit
the topic shortly.

## Healthy Detachment: The Transcultural Rebirth

It is thrilling business to a child, this coming alive to self
as what Joseph Campbell called "an innovating center" of
life's doings.[15] Much of the absorbing play of any boy or
girl's life is guided by bursts of self-awareness, by piercing
enthusiasms and wonderings: "Who am I?" "Who shall I
be?" and "Which 'I' is the real me?" Heeding love begins
with the spiritual musings that turn children toward their
truths. Eventually that truth helps them transcend what
appears to be their lot in life. One author admitted that
she spent her entire childhood pondering selected constraints, primarily gender-related. She believed, because
she was female, that the doors to authoring books would
be closed. But she became a viable writer as soon as she
transcended the limiting notions she'd adopted from her
culture.

In a moving account of the practical ramifications
of this transcendence *The Evacuation Diary of Hatsuye
Egami* describes one woman's daily efforts to transport
herself and her children beyond the inhumane, "extreme
situation." When first interned as a Japanese-American
prisoner of war in California, Hatsuye Egami and her
daughters were escorted to the public latrine, where
refinement and civility had no value. At first she felt

sick. Presently she realized that returning to a state of nakedness reveals people's true worth, so she told her daughters,

> I think that life here is going to be largely primitive and naked. But don't you think that this is interesting, too? All of you have been able to enjoy civilized life fully until now. Life cannot be interesting if only in one color. It is like a design created by variegated color strands woven together. It may be that in a naked life there is poetry and truth...from this bare life we can be something creative and interesting. The person that can do that is really intelligent and wise. Let's carve out a good life together.[16]

Inspired thought, with its infinite symmetry, compassion, and universal order, "makes the light shine in the darkness" (John 1:5). Only that illogical rebirth in Love gives us the ability to live with dignity, despite inhuman circumstances.

Elsewhere I've called this "social transcendence" a perceptual mode by which we separate or unplug from cultural conditioning. At its most profound, it spurs a rebirth by which we achieve oneness with divine consciousness, "the kingdom of God," unity-consciousness — the transcending of world opinion or the "mass mind."[17] Essayist and mystic Simone Weil believed that we escape the collective that is alien to everything sacred only by *rising above* the personal — the personality — and rooting ourselves in the impersonal good that is sacred.

In psychiatrist A. Reza Arasteh's work we read that the onset of intense periods of spiritual rebirth begin at around age two. These cycles repeat in adolescence, and recur during the "final integration" in adulthood. Arasteh dubbed the fully integrated awareness "rebirth in the transcultural state," proposing that wholeness demands healthy detachment from familial and societal ties, as well as separation from significant others.[18]

## Withdrawal as an Inspired Choice

During their critical stages of social and personal growth, most healthy children vividly experience their emotions. Here again, intensity of feeling can cause empathic, sensitive children to withdraw or to defend themselves against overstimulation through some sort of detachment. Need for emotional buffers could explain why the religiously gifted leave home early for cloistered settings and why, once there, their spiritual directors keep visits to and from family at a minimum.[19] A cloister is meant to offer minimal distractions, associates of kindred spirit, and an opportunity to feel less at odds with one's environment than in the mainstream culture where a longing for solitude is always suspect. Of course, not every solitary is introverted or "a loner."

Solitary, creative boys and girls may in fact be extroverts or have inordinate sympathy for their family's concerns. If they identify with others to an unproductive degree, they'll internalize a parent's or sibling's suffering as if it were their own. Their preferred introversion could be an inspired tactic to manage ultraempathy or the excessive pleasures of socializing that, left unchecked, undermine the spiritual realities they love most.

In our era of strident togetherness, few adults appreciate the vocational subtleties of single-minded youngsters who long to make something special or sacred out of their lives. The spiritually intelligent yearn for a wholly new orientation: to quit run-of-the-mill activities and trivializing pastimes. The movement of the Spirit within arouses even a very young child to tune into that hidden grace. In the case of inventive, religious, or artistic children, such inspirations might motivate the pursuit of contemplative pastimes that so easily confound others. Particularly, spiritually bankrupt adults are unable to accept solitary, meditative vocations as gifts of the highest order.

## Self-Trust as an Inspired Choice

When I was a school principal, not a few parents or teachers of, say, a budding designer or botanist felt upset with their child for liking to play alone. Typically, they thought nothing of visiting my office to insist that I zap their youngster out of the introverted engagement into a more "normal" extroversion. They were not above hounding pediatricians or pill-dispensing psychiatrists to prescribe curing tablets or therapies to "fix" (i.e., adjust) their young heretic. This seems an intrusion of the greatest magnitude and a theft of the child's vital life. The adult is out of step, not the child. Furthermore, each such act displays the adult's spiritual poverty. This is when we should hope a child's wisdom speaks loudly enough to spark some self-sheltering strategy so that the child can limit unwholesome compliance. Some show of protest is healthy. Positive rebellion is an attribute of spiritual intelligence and discussed at length later. For now, a few words about parenting styles that can thwart children's self-trust seem fitting.

Joel Kramer and Diana Alstad explore the vast divide between "parenting aimed at holding on to authority and the parenting that leads children to self-trust."[20] Whatever undermines self-trust is, over time, detrimental to wholeness. I liken strident, manipulative, or ultra-authoritarian households to child psychologist Bruno Bettelheim's "extreme situation." All such terms are relative, but powerless individuals, such as abused women or children, identify much too closely with the needs and the logic of their abusers. This identification is unsound. An overly agreeable little aspirant for a baby beauty-queen contest is too young to set limits for the adults surrounding her. She won't, or can't, question her right to "make waves." She will dutifully adorn herself with seductive make-up or scant clothing in order to please. Each compliant act leaves her more susceptible to that which undermines what intuitively she may know corrupts her best long-range interests. Rarely do submissive children escape or tell off controlling people or manage their abusers.

Bettelheim, who survived both Dachau and Buchenwald, believed that panic can be incapacitating.[21]

Adults often can't — or won't — figure out what's wrong in their relationship with their children. Their dullness (or denial) is part of everyone's problem. Some believe they've been fabulous supporters of a child, when in truth they are vulgar, crazed, or simply cruel and mean-spirited. Others blame a child for family upsets, ignoring their significant role in the turbulence. They expect children to be mature, but side-step their own immaturities. They employ clichés to promote a fictive "togetherness" ("The family that prays together stays together"). Or tell themselves "things will get better soon." That response smacks of the deer-caught-in-the-headlight syndrome: The situation is so disastrous that they freeze in place, cannot cope — even when their instabilities or neglect promise to drive away the child. In the worst case, this becomes the sadism that abuses unto death.

## Healthy vs. Unhealthy Securities

Bruno Bettelheim believed that overly compliant youngsters cannot fully participate in life because they've chosen an unproductive attachment to "the beloved mother."[22] They feel that it's wrong to leave, outdo, or "hurt" the reigning parent, and *that* is the true neurosis that can cause future failures for a child.

Sensing that a healthy separation is in the wind, some adults reinforce toxic attachments. They need to be needed more than they need to protect, nurture, or love their child. They ignore or defeat the child's small victories. Refuse to let girls and boys be individuals in their own right. Aggravate an offspring's guilt about leaving for college, marriage, or work. That pattern augments issues raised earlier: Adult insecurities, their projections or envyings rupture the healthy bonds they'd like to have with children.

When a child's success outshines an adult's, it may underscore the elder's ineptitudes. In that case, some parents drive their child away. They're mean, cranky, whiney. Or they cunningly subvert the youngster's independence. Or they underrate his or her chances for happiness. Misery does love its company. The inspired child is graced with the love that fathoms this and, for life's sake, leaves the ruinous nest.

## Learning from the Early Awakener: Heeding Love

Love's movement in and through the thought processes of children gives them the wit and bite to step out of harm's way. This is most clearly noticeable in saintly youngsters who reject a traditional family or narcissistic parents or convention's rule for their faith. We see that pattern repeatedly in creatively gifted boys and girls, like James Baldwin, who stay their course no matter who tells them to swerve. A reminder: In later life these same individuals may lose their way. Baldwin spent some tortured years as an adult. Still, my snapshot of what I view as his inspired thought illustrates that, at key points in a youth's life, we can see what it is like to be summoned, preoccupied, with a supernal love.

Perhaps in childhood few utterances of protest crossed your own lips. More early work: To locate in your shards of inconsistencies the optimism and, plainly put, the logic and language by which to structure your unique, yet thoroughly universal, life. This, too, is heeding love — the way by which you become well integrated, a true individual. And it's never too late to do that work. Adults ask, "How soon can we know what a child loves?" To find anyone's spiritual fingerprint seek out their all-consuming love — whatever animates their joy and rapt attention.

Boys and girls who can say yes and no with firmness to their absorbing delights ultimately define themselves. They say, "*This* is what I want, who I am, what I love."

Through words and tangible choices, they show us how to structure our most promising vocational options. For example, writer May Sarton's girlhood choices seemed to guard her integrity. What she thought, said, and did protected her own best interests. That's "heeding love." Sarton let others know who she was by her youthful decisions to shape her writer's life:

> From the time I was twelve years old, I was *dedicated* to writing; it was a *true* vocation. If you have that, I think you should think twice about marriage. I think that because I would take marriage very seriously and would feel I had to give a great part of myself to do it. Then, perhaps, I wouldn't have been able to do what I've been able to do.
>
> It's not that I'm against marriage. It's that I'm *for* the creative part of me which wouldn't be completely free if I were married.[23] [Italics in original]

Sarton's dedication to writing seems inspired. To me, her choice to remain single reveals intuitive authority, inner order, coherency — all the vital mental energy discussed. Sarton understood what she needed in girlhood. By contrast many of us, as adults, still cannot declare our purposes. We're indecisive, entrenched in convention, embarrassed to pursue our preferred delights, friendships, or careers.

Here is one rule of thumb: When we are struggling to follow the heart's leadings, it is essential to be compassionate with ourselves, to let intellect *serve* the heart — and appropriately. Reconsidering James Baldwin's story we'll see that in settings that discourage children's gifts, heeding love can be daunting. If in youth we were surrounded by people who failed to grasp who we were or what we needed, and if we were appeasing, then the tasks of our "early work" may linger with us into maturity.[24] My experience says it is risky to try to jump over these assignments en route to some goal. A persistent, subtle depression — sadness, inability to enjoy life — can follow us into adulthood without the completion of our elemental tasks.

Whatever our age, the unfolding inspiration reveals our heart's affections. Obstructions are strangely purifying, not all negative, and manageable. It's sometimes easier to know what we love when our path to it seems blocked. We reach out for the thing. We know we're on fire for it. Speaking out those truths, we'll feel emancipated. Not that we are precisely. There is no end to the ramifications of our finest liberty. Yet a profound vitality flows fresh from each authentic stretch and truthful utterance. In this we're all obliged to heed and speak the truths flowing from our deepest universal love. Or else, as Shakespeare warned, concealing that love, our heart will break,

> And rather than it shall, I will be free
> Even to the uttermost, as I please, in words.[25]

# Chapter Five

# Rising to the Occasion

*I love to be alone — in my car, parked somewhere
with a beautiful view. I write letters, read, or just re-
lax when I'm alone like this with my own thoughts.*
— Student, age sixteen

In childhood, Georgia O'Keeffe was teased about her
"crazy notions" but given wide latitude to speak her
mind. She did pretty much as she wished. She was self-
reliant, had her idiosyncrasies, dressed distinctively ("only
wearing white stockings . . . when her little sisters were not
wearing theirs"), was kept apart from other children and
her own siblings, and played alone as soon as possible.
Georgia's brothers and sisters were also allowed to be
"irresponsible individualists," for in the O'Keeffe family "the prevailing emotion was kindness and mildness."[1]
There are big lessons here.

The adult O'Keeffe readily tapped into the organizing vistas of her earliest inspirations. John Briggs tells
us that in maturity O'Keeffe remembered the exact hues
and patterns of a quilt she sat on as an infant: "a cot-
ton patchwork of two different kinds of material — white
with very small red stars spotted over it quite close together and black with a red-and-white flower on it. I was
probably 8 or 9 months."[2] Her words reveal ever-present

sensory data, the precise shades of light and colors, that she employed freely in later paintings. O'Keeffe's biographer Laurie Lisle notes that while Georgia was still playing with her dollhouse, she announced her intention to become an artist. Adults humored her ambitions, yet in her mind the term "artist" meant that she could "do as she wished." O'Keeffe "did not grow up feeling limited by her sex," and self-assurance developed "rather early."[3] While young she "calmly restated her conviction that God *was* a woman . . . and refused to accept the traditional role assigned to her by her gender."[4] Georgia O'Keeffe rose to the occasion of her life's creative challenge because her early nest somehow cultivated, or at least did not thwart, an able turn of mind. In this chapter we'll explore some factors that help us summon the wherewithal to rise to the occasion of demands. We'll also examine a few elements that may block our path to a capable way of being.

## Overview: Rising to the Occasion

Youth asks us to set our own stage for a constructive life. Imaginative proclivities and interests crop up in most children, particularly when an intellectually permissive climate stimulates their thinking. Giving children "intellectual liberty" does not mean random parenting. Strict parents with definite rules and clear values can still affect children positively. One way or another, a child's *subjective* life must flourish. Children need a bit of freedom during what's called "fantasy play" to build resourceful skills. In their re-creational, make-believing mind, they transcend limits, reveal likes and dislikes, and become individuals in their own right. It's as if their imagination orchestrates the future.

Eventually, children must move beyond pretending to learn how to translate the lessons of play into the demands of practical reality.

## The "Extreme Situation"

My mother's background may hold clues to the sort of trauma that thwarts healthy development. I know little about her childhood, so let me start with my experience. I was born in China during World War II. After the Japanese invaded and occupied China, I watched my father, an American entrepreneur, escorted at gunpoint by soldiers to what was euphemistically called an internment center. It was a concentration camp. Eventually most influential citizens who had ties to the Allied nations resided there. Why my mother was spared, I don't know. Some women were. Some weren't. Anyway, after that things at home began to sour.

My mother was left alone for the first time in her life. She had a toddler to raise (me) and a sprawling estate to manage while stranded in a volatile, alien land. I suspect she was emotionally unprepared to cope. My impression is that she lacked a firm "I am," a sturdy sense of self from which to forge a future or even to effectively protest. To be sure, she protested, but unproductively. To borrow a line from an old nursery rhyme, when things were good at home they were very, very good. When they were bad...well, you know how it goes.

From the time I was about three, my mother withdrew into what seemed a terrorizing netherworld. Over the years, her coherency faltered, and then took a nose-dive. Until she began to confuse me for herself, my life frolicked along as usual.

Being forced to endure what child psychologist Bruno Bettelheim called an "extreme situation" may have dismantled whatever fragile defenses my mother possessed. She was artistic, graceful — a kind of dreamy, intuitive person. It's likely she entered adulthood without proper internal supports. I'm told my mother was raised in an autocratic home and then a strict convent environment. Perhaps like Germaine Greer wrote years ago, the traits and functions that were wanted from my mother (and women of her generation) were those of the castrate — timidity, lessened power and vitality. This is pertinent. If conditions are such that we feel we must continually bow down to the collective, if we feel our life is governed by "insensitive, irrational, and overwhelming powers" or by people who seem to have total control over our existence, and who degrade our life, the "extreme situation" can cause serious instabilities.[5]

Ours was a genial live-and-let-live household. Everyone respected everyone else's little quirks and mostly treated each other's need for privacy or sociability with deference. Let's just say I had plenty of reflective elbowroom. For support I leaned on the host of attentive adults who lived with us, especially my grandmother and governess. Those two provided care, stability, and the intimacies required for childhood education.[6] Until around age six, I felt I had three mothers.

Thus all during the war while my mother continued to experience an "extreme situation," I kept my careful distance from her and lived in a fruitful world, developing my creative druthers.

## The Need for Privacy

Too many girls and boys crave solitude for it to be an eccentricity or an outgrowth of an unhealthy isolation or a chaotic household. Here's another case in point: Like Georgia O'Keeffe, Mahatma Gandhi preferred to play alone. He, too, had considerable contemplative freedom and rehearsed what was to be his adult role on boyhood's stage. He was painfully shy. Reading and reflection were his main companions. He may have luxuriated in a monastic studiousness. Each day after school Gandhi scurried home lest anyone speak to him. He "jealously guarded" his character, but teachers called him stupid for not copying spelling words from other boys' slates. (He said, "I never could learn the art of 'copying.' ")[7] By adolescence, Gandhi had set his own strict requirements for leisure time: He graced his playmates with his presence primarily when they gave him the leader's role.

One imagines a bony, sensitive, authoritative lad tucked away in his room, searching in books for life's largest truths and cultivating the determined philosophical stance that would so elegantly characterize his maturity. Psychoanalyst Erik Erikson writes that young Gandhi was famished for Truth and "already senses in himself early in childhood some kind of originality that seems to point beyond competition with the personal father."[8] Here we find a boy yearning for virtue of an uncommon, ineffable sort. Long after watching a theatrical production of one warrior's struggle for truth, he felt haunted, and repeat-

edly wondered why everyone couldn't be as virtuous as
the hero.[9]

Erikson reports that Gandhi's parents raised all their
children modestly, in "small, stuffy, and darkened rooms,"
but granted their son the ample freedoms he sought. He
loved to explore the outdoors. He dictated his own terms
and refused to be supervised during those adventures.
Gandhi is said to have been fearless when playing alone. He
appears to have been a domineering, forceful child. When
his father was absent from home, he assumed the role of
authority figure, sitting in his father's chair and barking
orders at others. In fact, Gandhi's first "nonviolent dissent" came in direct response to his mother's admonition
against some mischief of this sort. When involved with
other children, Gandhi enacted his chief passion, as the
peacemaker:

> He would never "play" unless he was in a position
> of such moral dominance that he could convince
> himself and others that the power game of his me-
> diatorship was "for their own good." And (not
> unimportantly) it often turned out to be just that.[10]

## Roots of "Rising to the Occasion": Self-Authority and Engagement

Instead of longing for, say, moral virtue, some children
cherish colors and light. Graphic artist Ben Shahn knew
in early childhood that he was an artist. He loved the
shape of letters and printmaking and telling stories with
his art. Ben Shahn learned in school that "it was a terrible
thing" to tell a story with a painting.

> It was the worst thing you could do. But I also had
> to face the fact that I liked to tell stories, ... whether
> in words or in pictures ... I had to face it.[11]

Inspiration and self-authority helped Shahn rise to the occasion of his need to separate from school norms. Young Ben knew the rules. Yet some impersonal force, the confident "I Am," pressed for distinction according to a higher, inner standard.

Other children love bugs or cooking or leadership tasks. Or they're obsessed with issues of justice. Aside from differing engagements their life process seems similar. Within their families and classrooms, even the shyest early awakener possesses a modicum of authority, if not outright leadership. These children shape their own realities. They commit themselves to recurring goals and values, much as adults do.

Absorption is a sign of inspiration. Early awakeners tend to be intense. Their entire existence seems an ongoing, perhaps ecstatic, struggle to externalize their hidden heart — what Shahn termed a "haunting inner image." For this reason, some children (and I was one) feel impelled to protect their creative space, their creative freedom. My bedroom was my sanctified domain. I hid in outdoor nooks. I never, not even as a child, accepted anyone else's interpretation of "laziness." Even while lounging about reading comic books, I felt industrious. I could be, and still am, downright rude if interrupted.

Most children who live in tight quarters convert their bedroom, bathroom, garage, or even the family car into a holy space. It is, for them, what church is for the devout: a sanctuary, a place of solace, a spot to breathe in deeply the air of private thought. Girls and boys who possess the physical space for privacy tend to develop a rich fantasy element in their play. They are "better able to concentrate, develop greater empathic ability and are better able to consider a subject from different angles...are happier, more self-assured, and more flexible in unfamiliar situations."[12] A sixteen-year-old I spoke to echoed:

> I love to be alone, usually when working on something....Because it's quiet, I get more done, like in the evening or late at night when nothing happens.

I loved to daydream and nightdream. Even more, I got exquisite pleasure from translating those fleeting mind-films into more durable forms: poems, stories, line-drawings, even little books and architectures that clarified my fantasies. My chief interest was building concrete models of my imaginative world with a construction toy. I can still feel and smell the little rubber bricks. While concocting anything, I did not wish to be disturbed. Unless my mother was on the prowl, I was left alone to do as I pleased. That was a blessing. And that's my point. For certain youngsters solitary play is essential. Pursuing the primary interest, they build competencies needed for later life.

O'Keeffe played alone, yet appears to have been a natural leader. Gandhi loved solitude and assumed the leader's role (another form of "aloneness"). In boyhood John Muir intuitively sought out solitude in nature. That habit may have kept him alive during years spent with an abusive father. His withdrawal mirrors an adult-like contemplation. Youngsters require emotional space and contemplative sanctuaries. For that matter, so do adults. Our myths of social adjustment and prescriptive "togetherness" force too many youngsters to fight for quiet time, to justify their love of privacy. This hurts everyone concerned.

## Roots of "Rising to the Occasion": Deep Thought and Continuity of Interest

A family friend of the late Supreme Court Justice Thurgood Marshall is quoted by his biographer as saying that as a youngster Marshall entertained sobering thoughts. "He was in deep study, that boy, and it was plain something was going on inside of him."[13]

When parents, siblings, or teachers intrude on this essential privacy, early awakeners may rebel. Their protests are generally a sign of sturdy spiritual health. They'll summarily reject adults if significant, stimulating *work* is being invaded. That "something going on inside" is a gainful employment. It provides a spiritual and creative wage (and not just for children). There is delight in figuring out — or "receiving" — answers to inherently beguiling puzzles. Insights derived from these youthful occupations produce cycles of relief and excitement, thus heightening the intensity of pleasure received.[14] Engrossments can lead to a vocation.

Dr. Vera John-Steiner concludes that gifted, inventive minds reveal "*continuity of concern*, intense awareness of one's active inner life combined with sensitivity to the external world."[15] While more average children may squelch their interests and fantasy play in favor of other people's priorities, inspired youngsters are true to themselves, staying immersed in favorite activities. They can become restless, feel empty, deprived, or unbearably frustrated "unless [expressing] the inner life in one or another creative way."[16] Innate preoccupations seem to help youngsters cope, intuit answers, organize and communicate complex ideas. For this, they have to remain engrossed. Sculptress Louise Nevelson sums it up:

> You have to be with the work, and the work has to be with you. It absorbs you totally and you absorb it totally. Everything must fall by the wayside by comparison.[17]

Good spiritual stewards provide the appropriate resources, reasonable structure (or discipline), and contemplative time to help the child follow a favorite line of inquiry. Then helpful adults move out of the way. This is another key. To repeat an old adage, the adult's main task is to nurture the young person's healthy independence, while responsibly working themselves out of a job. How can we stand on our own feet if we're "standing" by means of someone else?

### The Good "Spiritual Steward"

Most adults intuitively behave as productive mentors or good spiritual stewards of whatever talent seeks expression. They do so without "spoiling" children. We see this readily in parents who sacrifice time and money for flute, swimming, or skating lessons the instant they notice their offspring's fondness for such activities. The film *Searching for Bobby Fischer* portrays that spiritual stewardship through the parents of a pint-sized chess prodigy. Both mother and father help their son develop his exceptional gifts, trying not to inordinately pressure him. But perhaps especially the father wanted his son to win. The boy seems to view the game through playful, non-competitive eyes — as a friendly intellectual sharing, a dialogue of what works. We're shown how trouble brews if adults usurp, ignore, mismanage, or subtly misappropriate a child's talents. The sweetest-tempered girls or boys will fight for independence or become sullen and despondent if they feel their experience is being crushed. And why wouldn't they?

The healthier the child, the more astute will be the self-sheltering or defense mechanisms. For example, promising young leaders, gifted in the art of influence, are in the main self-governing. Their independence guards the talents over which they will retain control. They mull over daily challenges by themselves. They enjoy solving problems alone. They keep confidences, think deeply, initiate meaningful projects. Their autonomous preferences suggest they are structuring future capability. They even seem to know what skills they need for their adult contributions.

Some might wonder whether wanting to influence somebody is a spiritual trait. The answer all depends on the inborn flair. For those with leadership talent — like Saul, who became St. Paul — teaching, exhorting, and cerebral command of a domain are ways to self-actualize the gift. Joan of Arc confounds our stereotype of spirituality. Everyone with holy leanings need not mirror Florence Nightingale. If we compare any two dynamos of holiness, for instance, St. Augustine and Brother Lawrence, or Mother Teresa and Julian of Norwich, we readily see that spiritualities differ.

Then, too, if we're exploring inspired *thought,* then the mental side of spirituality will outweigh, say, the social. I have provided extensive data elsewhere that whole-seeing depends on cerebral functions — perceiving nondualistically, resolving paradox, seeing what could be as what is, synthesizing and conceptualizing, transcending paradigms, remaining open to nonconscious interior processes.[18]

Inspired thought (what I sense is the impress of the Holy Spirit on the mind and heart) kindles other inborn abilities. For someone with healing, parenting, or artistic prowess the outlets of inspiration are different than, say, for someone with peacemaking or evangelical drives. For the former, sharing-caring competencies may reign supreme. For the latter, communication-achievement-visioning skills might rule. Spiritual intelligence modifies both mind and heart. Yet whatever dominant Being-values we feel called to express will be accentuated, although of course an infinite, subtle array of other, complementary values will be honored in the process.

When a sixteen-year-old student described his sense of the matter, I felt he underscored the distinctive self from which his real strength would grow: "I'm a daydreamer. Often I find myself asking unusual questions in class. . . . My own questions interest me more than what's going on. I guess that's what makes me *me.*"

Singer k. d. lang always knew what she wanted. Today she believes:

It's not even an immodest thing. . . . It's like somebody saying, "I'm going to be a doctor." It's not a big deal.

The gestalt of lang's musical future seems to have been evident to her in her youth. Externals somehow helped consolidate, or inform, her inner experience:

> Every sort of information I got would be a huge thing for my fantasy life. An album cover would be like a movie — a whole other dimension I would travel in, like stepping through the looking glass. Everything I ever did was part of the development of my imagination and lust for discovering new cultures and new sounds.[19]

Spiritually intelligent children seek that intelligible self-renewal. They find ways to regenerate mentally and can face profound difficulty if parents (or others) set up repressive home and learning conditions. Paul Torrance, noted authority on youthful giftedness, lists five principles by which we can reward creative thinking — children's and our own:

- treat unusual inquiries respectfully,
- appreciate novel ideas,
- demonstrate that another's ideas have value,
- provide opportunities for self-initiated learning (and give credit for that when it occurs), and
- provide periods of nonevaluated learning.[20]

Torrance's list underscores the universality of the good guardianship of talent. We can and must grant children some immunity from oversupervision; we must let girls and boys initiate some projects and assume self-leadership in selected, appropriate activities. Reasonable autonomy in the area of expertise is essential, even for a child.

In a constricted milieu that is inhospitable to their interests, youngsters can become ill-mannered, even secretive. While it's critical to set high standards for learning and conduct (especially before age five) adults must intelligently place the child's needs, talents, and dictates for play before their own rigid rules and personal wants. This guideline poses a great challenge to the growing numbers of working parents who, of necessity, enroll their infants in preschool or leave them with virtual strangers. The use of institutional, "organized facilities" for childcare has increased by about 30 percent in recent years. An additional 22 percent of preschoolers are now cared for by nonrelative sitters. Only half of nearly ten million preschoolers are "watched by relatives while their mothers are on the job."[21] Instructional settings that nurture the whole child (and therefore spiritual intelligence) seem the ones to champion.[22]

### *Learning from Early Awakeners: Rising to the Occasion*

Adversity offers broad opportunities for developing spiritual competence. Encountered productively, the early trial is an early engagement. Handled wisely, it unfolds a point of view, possibly a lifelong theme to be pursued — an "occupation." If, in childhood, you find ways to influence your circumstances, you tend to develop interactive potency and judgment skills so critical to later life. And you'll derive those benefits ahead of your more pampered, sheltered friends whose parents rush in to settle every conflict for them. You'll structure independent thinking skills if you think things through on your own, and if your elders

- encourage your self-respect and self-sufficiency,
- give you latitude to make choices,
- grant you permission to stretch your mind's ability to "play" with concrete reality,
- let you grapple with occasional hurts and mishaps.

Then life's trials or sorrows won't harm you. At least not permanently.

If as children we failed to rise to the occasion of resourcefulness, we'll require lots of homework in that area as adults. To flourish, we need an "open," feeling heart and also a practical edge of capability. Observing the triumphant people in our midst — of almost any age — we see that they'll find

- language or coherent expression to give shape to their ideas,
- appropriate interpersonal skills,
- a positive, wholesome vision of what *could* be,
- the self-respect, self-trust, and optimism that productivity requires.

Self-pacing is also critical. For instance, youngsters will negotiate with their teachers more effectively about low grades when they're encouraged, not pressured, to speak up. They'll buck the tastes of the crowd and, for better or worse, will express themselves most freely in their dress if they feel ready to do so. The helpful principle for "rising to the occasion" is that our own self-respectful timing and courageous acts contribute to our effectiveness and cultivate traits such as

- confidence,
- a spiritual point of view,
- a capable turn of mind and firm sense of "I Am,"
- respect for intuitive experience, the "small, still voice" within.

Small, self-defining choices help us honor life. When self-respect demands action, we'll stretch with growing confidence into mastering a difficult day — or decade — of work or family disruption.

After all, you may not *feel* attractive, lovable, or worthwhile, but if you sense you have what it takes to survive, if you've observed yourself thinking clearly or have somehow protected your lucidity in minor matters, you can usually save your sanity, integrity, and intuitive experience in the long run. To gain that self-sheltering resourcefulness all children — all people — require:

- permission (and provisions) to express basic needs, to assert themselves, especially to give voice to dreams, fears, or anger — the subjective life,
- freedom to pursue their interests in their own way and at their own pace, and
- freedom to make and learn from so-called mistakes.

We adults so often pay lip service to the importance of learning from error, but nag and browbeat ourselves after a faux pas or scold youngsters who experiment too freely. Or we berate ourselves for feeling vulnerable. A fourteen-year-old I spoke to gave us this advice:

Try to understand your kids — what they want, what they're about as people. And just chill when a kid trips up.

So it was with me. In early childhood intense feelings — joy, a sense of religious elation, and terrible dark fears, too — framed an enduring question, namely, "What does it take to live a creative, emotionally healthy life?" My search for answers eventually led to safety, to a vocation, and to a spiritual perspective. Sometimes I had the luxury of self-pacing. But mostly not.

After we left China for the United States, my parents' undoing happened right before my eyes. One day there they were: two vivacious, gifted urbanites, leading a chic existence, providing me with every conceivable advantage, including love. The next day, or so it seemed, there they weren't. My mother took her leave emotionally, and my father took his physically after a massive heart attack. When the fictive gates protecting childhood swung open, I entered a stunning independence. On today's side of yesterday's trial, I tell you frankly: It wasn't too bad. It was thrilling, really.

# Chapter Six

# Choosing the Best Option

*When I was in third grade, I begged and begged my mother to buy me these espadrille shoes. She gave in. The shoes fell apart the minute I wore them. Then I begged her to return them for me. She made me handle that. She did that a lot: I had to solve problems with my teachers or playmates before she'd enter the scene. She'd say, "We can fix things for you, but we want you to speak up first."*

— College student

Close to the time of her death, an adolescent Anne Frank wrote these grounding words to herself: "I've found that there is always some beauty in life — in nature, sunshine, freedom, in yourself; these can all help you. Look at these things, then you find yourself again, and God, and then you regain your balance."[1]

In a wholly different era and circumstance, a three-year-old John Muir soothed himself with the healing properties of simple farming chores and nature. Boyhood included continual mistreatment by his father. A radical inner compass guided him to nature's sanctuary. His impulse to solitude and the outdoors was spiritually conceived and brought into expression. These outlets buoyed Muir's spirits and in time he transcended his peculiar "extreme situation." Intuiting what he needed for the good life, Muir chose it.

Spiritually intelligent children solve practical problems by moving beyond a wishful idealization of a virtue like courage to actually *being* courageous. They feel afraid and step out anyway. But what furthers and, conversely, what prevents us from choosing our various spiritual alternatives?

## Overview: Choosing the Best Option

This chapter suggests that, in part, selected behaviors — solitary, meditative play, productive uses of fantasy, and age-appropriate levels of personal authority — can cultivate real-life effectiveness. Youngsters who learn to acknowledge their fears, shyness, or other constraining feelings, discerningly work around these. As one boy told me, "Just because I feel something doesn't make it real." In separating disruptive feelings from our higher thoughts and values, our best options become apparent.

A best option for one may not be "best" for another. With increased spiritual intelligence, a philosophic day-dreamer may gravitate to whatever lets her gaze out of windows. She'll converse with mentors who comprehend and value novel, abstract thought while a potential dancer exhibits kinesthetic drives. The one thing you notice about such youngsters is that they don't check their opinions or inclinations at the door.

Beneficent dreams, a hunch, or, as in Muir's case, a feeling of what (or who) will soothe prompts children to turn toward certain friends, the outdoors, or a favorite grandparent. They seek out enrichment from pets, music, or a folk tale. In all cases, vital mental energy is a foundation for wholesome growth, the ability to spot — or create — options. A healthy imagination introduces children to the promise of their future, especially as it reveals their own meanings, helps them trust their instincts and bring those into play. Some hardship (sometimes more than an appropriate amount) turns the spiritually inclined back to themselves.

The poet Rainer Maria Rilke suggested that perhaps everything terrible is in its deepest being something helpless that wants help from us.[2] In this sense, children learn to use their inner world creatively as they find the constructive power of some holy (whole) ideal, stretch with mind and heart into compassion or risky but meaningful aims and forgiveness, even love, for whatever initially seems hostile.

Whatever dominant Being-values the spiritually intelligent feel summoned to express through work or relational life will be accentuated in their best choices. Two examples may explain what I mean.

## Choosing the Being-Values: Justice

If one intends to champion the rights of others, an appropriate level of assertion is required. Thurgood Marshall's family encouraged that. His great-grandfather was a slave, "one mean man," of such defiance and ferocity that he could not be sold. His owners finally set him free on the proviso that he leave town and never return. Marshall's grandparents and parents were social activists who routinely demonstrated pride in their heritage. Although he was a timid preschooler, around age five Marshall experienced a turning point. No one knows exactly what caused his change, but he toughened up. His father, "the most insidious" of the family's protestors, further influenced Thurgood's rebellion. Father taught son how to argue, how to employ logic for each point he wanted to prove, "even if we were discussing the weather."[3] Once after a street brawl in which a stranger branded the young Marshall with a racial slur, his father commanded him to fight if anyone ever insulted him again.[4]

In Thurgood Marshall's case, parental coaching seems to have furthered a passion for justice. In Muir's case, time spent in nature and alone conveyed the mentor's spirit.

Wise, protective adults realize that children need a taste of real-world difficulty to learn what life's about. The thoughtful university student quoted at the opening of this chapter credited both parents for teaching her to be assertive: "They sort of forced me to solve problems, but gently." She's noticed that some of her friends nearly ready to graduate call home about every little upset, expecting their parents to intervene. Today, she's grateful for her upbringing:

> We children expressed ourselves at the dinner table. My father came home from work, exhausted. But he listened. My falling off my bike, or whatever, was just as important as his work. We all discussed our feelings and opinions honestly.

## Choosing the Being-Values: Holiness

Choice-making patterns of religiously gifted children in the Middle Ages suggest that the inner call to a life of

worship is distinct by about age seven. Bell and Weinstein
found that girls with saintly tendencies heard their "call
to holiness" or asceticism before adolescence. Typically,
a religious girl rejected the usual socialization, especially
the choices of her mother, who provided the standard
feminine model against which to rebel.[5] Understandably,
parents couldn't fathom where their daughters got such
ideas. Had a service such as psychiatry been available,
business would have been brisk. Not only the explicitly
virtuous or traditionally "good" child strives for holiness.
Sometimes the rebel is a would-be saint.

If we adults learn to listen actively, attentively, to children, we more easily hear their yearning for holiness.
Psychiatrist Robert Coles mentors us in that art by offer-
ing us page after page of rousing, in-depth interviews of
spiritually intelligent children of all types. One eight-year-
old, Connie, intrigued Coles with her blunt, idiosyncratic
views about orthodox religion. Deeply spiritual, she did
not want to become "a religious." As Coles explains,

> Some people, she declared, even children her age,
> were "more religious than the priests and nuns."
> ...She let me know that the rebellious side of
> Jesus had not escaped her notice, and that in Berna-
> dette of Lourdes and Joan of Arc she admired young
> Catholic women whose virtues, whose important
> spiritual lives, were not at all acceptable to es-
> tablished Catholic authorities. Most important, she
> let me know that her religious life was far more
> many-sided than I had been prepared to admit.[6]

Connie wanted Coles to hear *her* truths, to become
less clinical in his observations. In turn he, being an em-

pathic listener, got "seriously involved in her religious discussions."[7]

In sum: Pedestrian households produce sensible, highly intuitive boys and girls, quite capable of making adult-like decisions and conversing about their inner life. The reality they deem sacred is a productive sheltering guide and a directive power.

Every child wonders, "Who am I, down deep? Who do I want to be? What do I value? What becomes of someone like me?" Youngsters rehearse their character's functions on the basis of their observations, beliefs — and inspirations. When they choose well, they bring their ambitions to life. Feelings of continual estrangement, profound enough to impede any adult, cannot thwart such children's intentions.

### Personal Patterns

Apart from my grandmother, my most productive mentors came from outside the family. By age six or seven I no longer recognized my mother. Whereas in the old, good days she had been loving and tender as a doe, now she was a wasp, buzzing furiously and unpredictably to keep you away. Once stung, you kept your distance. My kindest options seemed insincere and glossed over the real issue: Her symptoms frightened me. I would not tell her that. For one thing, she did not want to know. For another, I could not insult the gentle soul she really was. I accommodated myself with one simple vow: I'd care for myself, no matter what that required. Choosing to protect my grain of feeling made all the difference.

Evasions came variously: I shrugged off intimacies, left

the family scene, was rude, or stayed with friends. Parents of school chums, aware of my dilemma, helped. After my father died, good fortune sent a crusty poker pal of his to become my closest confidant. Never mind a huge age difference. He was my ersatz father, my childhood's best friend. As I'd had more than one mother, so had I a surrogate dad. I handled my emotions, marginally, by talking with him and by reassuring myself. I read voraciously. Watched people. Asked questions. Made friends. Adopted my friends' parents — as needed. I lived in my mind. That aggregate solution let me size up who could be trusted. The discovery that not just blood relatives were reliable mentors generated a cautious optimism.

## Precursors of Wholesome Choice-Making

I'm not saying that a child will function optimally if brutally treated or lacking in external support. However, we all know that emotional buttressing can come from outside the home, for instance, from a caring teacher or a therapist with the intuitive sensibilities of a Robert Coles. Decidedly, shoring up can and must flow from *within* the child. Inspired thought is spiritually instigated. It grants early authority.

The spiritually intelligent may possess a strong self-image. Or not. They may "feel good" about themselves. Or not. They may, as I did, seek an early independence by disengaging emotionally from an elder who frightens, suffocates, abuses, or manipulates them. Or not. Autonomy may blossom in the twinkling of an eye, or develop gradually. They'll display bold intent and zany humor. Or be timid. Or grave as stones. They might feel enthused.

Or depressed, nearly asphyxiated by their troubles. The one constant that sparks healthy drive and constructive choices is a vital subjective life. The inspired child derives self-respect and a cluster of synergistic resources, for instance:

- productive mentors,
- vital mental energy,
- productive inner cues, like discernment and a constructive imagination,
- purity of heart, or virtue, which *is* power.

## Productive Mentors

Any empathic individual who cares for us, has faith in us, and whose reliable affection sustains us, can ignite self-trust and courage.[8] These attributes produce the "good feelings" we hear so much about today: self-esteem, the sense that we are loveable, powerful, deserving, and worthwhile. If someone we respect believes in us, it's easier to believe in ourselves. It's that faith that sharpens our best choice making.

Not all mentors — guides or teachers — are "elders."[9] Age-mates can mentor each other. A touching illustration of sibling support is shared by Gavin De Becker. He and his sister ran away from home one night to avoid the brutality of their mother, "an intelligent, funny, well-read, and beautiful woman — and a heroine addict." After stopping at an all-night market, they anonymously phoned the police about "kids loitering" and then waited for the police to cart them off to jail. They chose their best option out of two grisly alternatives, as De Becker notes:

They could hardly put a twelve-year-old boy and a fourteen-year-old girl in with hardened criminals (though we might have felt at home), so they put us in our own cell. In the morning, we called our grandfather, who picked us up and took us home. Two kids found bruised and red-eyed and panting at three-thirty in the morning and nobody asked us a thing. It was as if the police saw these dramas every day, and I know now that they do.[10]

Sometime later, the two collaborated to modify a bedroom window-screen for easy escape, if need arose. Their survival gambits vividly depict a collaborative survival mechanism fostered by keen imagination and the will to prevail. In *Protecting the Gift,* De Becker calls intuition "the source of safety." Inspired thought (the prompt to creative action) and intuition (a revelation or truth derived by insight) are intimately linked.

In childhood the self-respect that lets us choose options in line with our inspirations seems to require a precursor: unconditional love from at least one person whom the child respects and whose affection the child can rely on and/or learning resourcefulness. I define that resourcefulness as the ability to learn how to learn what's of value, and the leverage skills to apply what's learned. We are resourceful learners when we can translate what we've gleaned into practical action. Youngsters who sense they have the resourcefulness to deliver the goods tend to perform well under pressure.

Productive mentors help children *earn* their good feelings through their actual accomplishments — say, by fostering a rebound after disappointments or by helping them stand up to a tyrant or ask for what they need. Mentors furnish much-needed reality-based feedback, not fictional praise. Productive mentors, by definition, affirm the life-force of others.[11]

Blessed are the children who are touched by just one spunky adult who confers permission to feel or give constructive voice to a healthy range of emotions. Inhibited, oversocialized children typically don't find words or appropriate choices to express their feelings. They thwart themselves by

- burying so-called negative responses such as anger and jealousy,

- telling themselves their goals don't count,

- picturing themselves as unworthy; no utterance of need, anguish, or irritation passes through their lips.

The study of "invulnerables" — children who flourish despite trauma — suggests that boys and girls who become exemplary adults are skillful shapers of their relationships, because they trust themselves enough to locate productive adult support. They'll form a bond with at least one reliable grown-up — like a friend's parent, a teacher, a relative, or a neighbor. As mentioned, those who endure some cataclysmic eruption may need to revisit their early unrest later, with a trustworthy therapist or spiritual director. It could be that, in childhood, they begin that work by "exploiting" some caring relationship to survive a childhood ordeal with, say, a violent or mentally ill parent or extreme poverty.[12] However, the least complicated relationships also can enhance spiritual intelligence.

A friend now in her fifties fondly recalls a chambermaid as being the first (and only) adult to forward the idea that women's work could be liberating. Her comments tell us that helpful relationships can be temporary and exceedingly informal. At age five, my friend and her parents had vacationed for a week at a summer resort. While changing sheets and scouring the tub, the housekeeper befriended the child with a running narrative about the importance of having something worthwhile to do in life. That was an eye-opener:

> Each day, for five days straight, the maid had me thinking about work. Before that, I'd had no inkling that a woman could have a job, earn money, be active outside her home. I'd never entertained a reality of work as having a rightful place in *my* future. That woman took time to educate me. She *looked* at me: really saw me, listened to my remarks. I'll never forget her.

Children thrive on stories that structure both realistic and fanciful images in their minds. They love to hear and rehear family lore that depicts their ancestors' prowess. Conversations that help children envision a worthwhile future may define or outline actual challenges. Those discussions let a youngster rehearse constructive responses and prepare the character structure they hope one day to have.

Meaningless patter that centers on the adult ("Let me tell you how it was for me when I was your age"), or platitudes that try to put children at ease or keep them at bay ("You're too young to worry about that") deprive boys and girls of reality testing. How can we consider our best options if we can't prepare inwardly for the roles we must or want to play?

## Vital Mental Energy

Vital mental energy seems coexistent with spiritual intelligence. It's the mentality we adopt for meeting life. As we think in our hearts, Scripture informs us, so we are (Prov. 23:7). Vital mental energy is a spark plug for...

- hope,

- drive, spunk, or *animation* — the breath of life (and it's the same breath in men as it is in women),

- subjective power — not derived from externals (e.g., praise, rewards).

In her biography of Eleanor Roosevelt, Blanche Wiesen Cook deftly examines vital energy, primarily in women. She suggests that historically we've ignored "the essential mysteries of a woman's life," and she asks,

> How do we channel energy — to write, to organize, to love? How do we acquire courage, develop vision, sustain power, creative style? What is the connection between chronic undiagnosed illness, depression, suicide and the refusal to acknowledge the fullness of a woman's capacities, her right to love and to lead?[13]

I propose that both girls and boys derive vital mental energy, endurance, and sane, edifying commitments from a mode of inspired thought that honors the core

self with its delights. Whoever is established in a healthy
emotional and relational life is edified from within. That
means children must discern how to accept, express, and
manage their thoughts, their aggression, their reliance
on others, their invigorating or devitalizing influences.
(Surely we all know at least one "too nice," ineffectual,
ever-appeasing sort who simply lacks the will — or common sense — to flourish.) The "extreme situation" is a
dark principality that drains away the vital mental energy that is positive faith, which might otherwise help us
choose our best options, thereby rising to the occasion
of our need. Briefly, we review some of what undermines
that capacity.

### What Retards Vital Mental Energy?

Repeatedly, Bettelheim observed childhood schizophrenia
evolving out of conditions wherein a girl or boy was
convinced that life was being threatened by destruction
and that "no personal relations offered any protection
or emotional relief."[14] He believed young schizophrenics
feel about themselves and their life "exactly as the concentration camp prisoner felt about his."[15] Deprived of
hope, they both believe they lack authority and control
over their simplest choices. They feel at the mercy of de-
structive, irrational forces that seem bent on exploiting
or harming them:

> Under such conditions the egos of most people
> are unable to give protection against the devastat-
> ing impact of the external world; they are unable
> to exercise their normal tasks of assessing reality

correctly or predicting the future with reasonable accuracy, thus making it impossible to take steps to influence it.[16]

In such cases, vital mental energy is unavailable either for investing in one's inner life or for controlling externals. This observation makes the insights and compassion of a girl like Anne Frank seem all the more inspired.

An adult's manipulation or harangues can transform the innocence of youthful play into guilty pleasures. Browbeaten children feel like they're avoiding their "duty" when they're daydreaming or gazing in awe at the sky. These nondoing activities, these contemplative slices of life, incalculably nourish developmental processes. Controlling adults frequently disable a child's *self*-control. The parents' voices are

- always "on,"
- forever stressing rules,
- calling attention to their adult needs, wants, pain, fury,
- placing their own concerns at center-stage of the family dynamic.

Youngsters must listen to the adult, not to their inward voice. They forget to honor and eventually discount their inner cues. The inept, weak, resigned, or chronically ill may wield despotic clubs, too — not just the strident. Domination of every sort forces everyone in a household to pay homage, but not to their own still, small voice.

Like stage-parents who hope for their own glory through their offspring's achievement, some adults exploit children's gifts for private purposes, but intuitive children instinctively shy away from exploitation. That, too, is a best option.

Parents who resent or dislike their spouses may also subvert children's vital mental energy. They tell tales "out-of-school" about their partner and weigh down the youngster with way too much intimate data. They forge an unhealthy bond with the child. They nit-pick. The movie *Mother* depicts this phenomenon humorously when a writer returns to his boyhood home to live with his mother. He hopes to unearth the reason for his creative blocks — in work and love. We're shown that his troubles are rooted in early feelings that he could never please Mom. Although his mother has chucked the past and moved on, he's locked in a dysfunctional time warp. That's his problem, not hers.

A "mommy's boy" might become frail, sickly, and full of pent-up resentment. Frequently he considers his body as his mother's "temple," becoming finicky and guilt-ridden if he does not properly protect that sacred structure.[17] He may be passive, avoid adventure, become friendless or enraged. "Daddy's girls" easily relinquish their own life for their father's. Overconcerned, they nurse their father too intimately in his old age. Or they strain to be the son Dad wanted but never had. High achievement and caretaking drives are laudable attributes unless they corrupt an individual's wholesome nature. If so, vital energy coils inward. After too many years of, say, counterfeit caretaking the child's healthy independence is hindered. As a later chapter suggests, a psyche that's been poisoned by years of noxious supervision easily evolves a self-sabotaging reflex.

Alert, inventive — yes, even rebellious — individuals learn to

- consider their own needs,
- develop an intuitive, self-protective reflex,
- verbalize or somehow take seriously their desire for empathy and care.

They spot and use any escape hatch — psychological or physical — to detach themselves (at the very least, emotionally) from inept or misbehaving grown-ups. Earlier, Connie's example showed some youngsters are amazingly perceptive in this regard. When parents, siblings, teachers, or others try to undermine or intimidate them these more boisterous children establish clear boundaries.

### Productive Inner Cues: Discernment

Sufficiently self-possessed boys and girls reveal the significance of relying on hunches, gut feelings, our survival instincts. Ultimately, such children will agree with playwright Robert Bolt, who, through his hero for all seasons Sir Thomas More, noted that God made us to serve him wittily, "in the tangle of his mind! . . . Our natural business lies in escaping."

> God made the *angels* to show him splendor — as he made animals for innocence and plants for their simplicity. But man he made to serve him wittily, in the tangle of his mind! . . . No doubt it delights God to see splendor where he only looked for complexity. . . . Our natural business lies in escaping.[18]

A child must frequently escape from too much so-called love, which is personal in the extreme: unwanted, smothering attention; unsolicited advice; misguided concern. Such predilections can truncate self-initiative.

We might entertain the quaint idea that saintly children eagerly accept parental misbehavior, seeking martyrdom. Perhaps we've concluded that it is God's will for someone to suffer or that the devout child looks for just rewards in heaven. This is unlikely. Surprisingly, the more divinely inspired the child, the sooner he or she cuts the umbilical cord of dependency — on family or any "special" overly personal relationship. Not for nothing did Jesus warn us that no one approaches the divine anointing without severing special attachments.

The religious child is hungry for an impersonal or nonpersonal or universal, superordinate compassion. Values, native intelligence, relational gifts, the hunger to create or to know God in the other or to share a talent with abandon — these factors spur investment in the long-haul difficulty or perilous choice that we call a "bitter cup." Be assured that saintly boys and girls walk out the door of even the most loving, nurturing homes if their religious vocation is profound enough. The choice to exit has less to do with the parents than it has to do with the movement of the Spirit.

### Purity of Heart

Weinstein and Bell render a touching account of the French hermit and eleventh-century saint, Theobaldus. When he was an adolescent doing battle with his caring parents, Theobaldus decided to pattern his life after the prophet Elijah and John the Baptist. His parents were set against his leaving home. The boy triumphed. Recorded family testimonies include a poignant interview between father and son, as relevant as if the exchange were taking place today:

> Father (tearfully): Son, why do you run away? This is your father you are fleeing, not the devil. I don't want to recall you from your vocation, but I am happy to have seen you, to have spoken with you directly even if only to see my son reject his grieving parents.

> Theobaldus (unmoved): Sir, don't upset me. Go in peace and let me remain in peace, in the peace of Christ.[19]

A sculptor told me that if her parents had not been so confused, she would not have spent her time alone in her room, creating art. The famed photojournalist Margaret Bourke-White believed another sort of adversity furthered her life. She idolized her engineer father who "was essentially the inventor and researcher, and made some unsound investments along the way." When her father died and financial trouble hit, Bourke was seventeen and just beginning college. She later wrote, "If we had been wealthy and I hadn't had to work my way through college as I did after his death, I would have never been a photographer."[20]

The spiritually intelligent, like Bourke-White, respect themselves enough to commit to doing the best they can in a given situation. These are our "little old souls," as evidenced by Theobaldus, who seem to possess an available, impersonal drive to succeed. They are simultaneously more vulnerable and more independent than their less animated but equally intelligent peers.[21]

Medieval stories portray the typical religiously gifted child as having virtuous, religious parents. These elders nurture the offspring's sacred sensibilities. There are a few colorful exceptions, tales about worldly parents with fixed expectations: Their child *will* live and marry conventionally, and to hell with the vocation. Unlike Theobaldus's father, who wanted only good for his son, these parents' goal is to wrest their child away from God so that the child will wed and work as they did.

Not every child rejects overbearing parents. Not every dominating adult damages a child. Overbearing parents — provided they are stable, caring, and responsible — may bequeath great self-confidence to a child and the optimism to fuel a lifetime's achievement. F. Scott Fitzgerald said that until he was fifteen his smothering mother helped him feel like there was nothing else in the world of importance except himself. In one study, roughly 64 percent of the parents of gifted, high achievers were both "dominating" (i.e., paying excessive attention to the child's career and future) and "smothering" (i.e., paying excessive physical or overprotective attention to the child).[22]

A few children dedicate themselves to overbearing (or dependent) parents. They appreciate the adult's better nature rather than concentrating on flaws. Not all youngsters possess that temperament. We will presently explore how children with a creative or religious makeup often separate emotionally from all but vocational influences. Their best option could be to shield themselves from special relationships of every sort.

## Learning from Early Awakeners: Choosing the Best Option

The spiritually intelligent learn to meet concrete demands. Some are "invulnerables" who must survive distressing circumstances. Others, like saintly children — or perhaps predominantly artists, inventors, or mystic types — display a level of intuitive artistry that sizes up and selects the optimal alternative. One decides on a night in jail rather than spend another at home with an unstable, abusive parent. Another determinedly runs off to a monastery. If summoned forth by a powerful vitality, a child will dig within, head out on a mythic journey, or, like Theobaldus, take risks to defend his or her life's purposes.

The spiritually intelligent teach us that best options are diverse, suited to our unique, superordinate intentions, and most readily available to adults who

- cultivate the vital mental energy that spots options,
- retrench and reject whatever threatens to undermine the core self,
- use and trust unseen, "irrational" forces,
- choose what works (instead of merely dreaming about it),
- forge a bond with reliable, supportive others.

That will to *choose* such wholesome paths, that inspired thought, that vital wit is power. It also is love, precisely as Meister Eckhart explained: Whoever has more will has more love, "So long as God lies hidden in the soul's ground."[23]

# Chapter Seven

# Early Artistry

*I'm someone who wants to experience as much of life as possible. My ideas are original. While I love gaining knowledge and insights from others, I emulate no one. I keep an open mind to new possibilities. I never limit myself in any way.*

— Student, age sixteen

A graduate student explained to me how it happened that, at age thirteen, he planned to kill himself:

> I was depressed. I felt so different from any of my friends. I wasn't a sports fanatic, wasn't destined for business like other guys. Then I had a vision: I was dead and lying in my coffin. But no one came to my funeral. The hall was empty. That made me mad. When I woke up the anger I'd turned inward, against myself, surfaced. "I'll show them," I thought. "I'll be a successful artist."

That boy's self-sheltering reflex was stimulated by acknowledging his anger and helped him accept his feelings. As he told me, "Insight gave me energy, self-confidence, and new-found self-respect." Insight prompted his constructive action. He told his parents what he'd been

112

feeling. They listened. They enlisted the help of a competent therapist. They counseled him themselves. Over the next months, the young man's father verbalized a powerful, unconditional regard:

> Do whatever you must to be happy. When I see fire in your eyes as you speak about art — creating your art — that sight makes me rejoice.

The young man said that sentiment helped most.

To overcome despair or harsh self-criticism youngsters may need to manage their family, their friends, even the sense of being too different to merit love. They'll need to overcome peer pressure or school problems. It's been shown that about 60 percent of the high achievers have faced serious challenges at school, three out of five disliked it, and four out of five evidenced some sort of superior gifts.[1]

Poet Rabindranath Tagore found his course work an unbearable torture. He quit school at age fourteen, saying the curriculum dissected his life into dead, symmetrical boxes.[2] A contemporary fourteen-year-old expressed the same thought in ordinary slang when he told me, "I wish adults knew that school sucks." (Most creative adults do know from first-hand experience.) Edison couldn't concentrate on commonplace studies. School officials called him impossible to teach. Ultimately he was ousted from school and tutored at home. As an Italian schoolboy, Pope John XXIII was "once sent home with a note to his village priest 'begging him to reprove the boy for not being conscientious about his studies and always [arriving unprepared].' The boy, however, suspected the contents of the note and did not deliver it."[3]

Sometimes it's not study per se but the interests we'd prefer to study that conflict with our elders' plans. Mick Jagger quit the London School of Economics to pursue music full time. When he first joined the Rolling Stones, Jagger reported that his father was "absolutely furious":

> Anything but this. He couldn't believe it. I agree with him. It wasn't a viable career opportunity. It was totally stupid. But I didn't really like being in college — It wasn't like it was Oxford and had been the most wonderful time of my life. It was really a dull, boring course.[4]

## Overview: Early Artistry

Artistry is an attribute of the Spirit. Possessing a private aesthetic, we know what we admire and need. Researcher Michael M. Piechowski found that gifted children had a sharp awareness of their issues of personal growth. They anticipated and prepared themselves for what was to come. One twelve-year-old told him:

> I think about what I am going to do when I get older. They are good thoughts. I seem to want to rush into life.... I fantasize about people I will meet in the future, places I will visit, friends I will make, where I will live.... I dream about being an adult.... It's sort of funny how us children dream about being older, and dream about the future and the adults dream about the past and being young again.[5]

An educator friend talks frequently with his college students about such challenges. He says they're puzzled by the variables of their own gifts, evidencing well-documented patterns of concern like

- what having "gifts" entails,
- why their elders expect them to be flawless in all things,
- why it's so difficult to find friends who empathize and accept them as they are,
- how to reconcile the feeling that one is too different or gets overwhelmed by one's own talents and abilities.[6]

The Bible warns us to abandon treasures that turn to dust and to store up riches that lead to life. Given our earthly obligations, our need for cash to pay for Big Macs, rent, and health insurance, this advice seems nonsensical. However, if we, like early awakeners, develop our inner wealth before bowing down to our gods of circumstance, we too can move beyond mere "IQ" in effectiveness. In that case, our gifts tend to serve both self and others. Spiritually intelligent children intuitively recognize that serving self and others requires the cultivation of rudimentary, indwelling capacities including:

- choosing-and-arranging artistry,
- self-sheltering artistry,
- demonstrated maturity,
- power to follow love,
- sacrificial disciplines, and
- ability to follow inner cues.

## *Personal Patterns*

A family member once recalled that when I was four I expressed a wish to live alone on a farm to raise horses. Before the first grade, my fever for constructing little projects clashed with family expectations. I was supposed to take a tepid, plodding pace but felt an electric intensity. Today I sense that keenness is universal, not a gender issue at all. I had a burning temperament, restlessness, a sense of determination, even urgency, to externalize something sacred sensed within. I knew (and pictured) exactly what I wanted, but had no adequate reply when my mother would beseech me, "Why must you get so excited?"

Why indeed? Why, when intention and excitement stirred up trouble, did one plunge herself, heart first, into mighty objectives and want to do things just so — precisely as envisioned beforehand? I learned much later, from a book about Ben Shahn, that artists of all sorts have a ferocious fondness for imprinting certain lovely images — their core truths — onto externals.

Intellectual stimulation was a given in our home. I was free to dream big dreams, to consciously use books, movies, the lives of family friends and self-told stories to explore life's exciting prospects. But the upheavals in our family left me knowing that I would soon design a way to leave home. That more abundant life was beckoning.

By age seven matters on the home front worsened. I routinely daydreamed of escape and craved the preexisting harmony of love — God — in the sense that Pascal suggested: Seeking the ineffable would not have occurred if God were not already a living reality. By age eight, I'd concluded the obvious: Material possessions, however agreeable, were insufficient for enduring bliss. Don't get me wrong, wealth was important to me (especially after my father died). Naively, I just assumed money followed certain holistic basics: vitality, self-respect, creative purpose, and sound mental health.

Whenever I met or read about admirable others who possessed such traits, they also had a firm grip on reality. Mentally, I documented those observations. My champions walked their talk. They were my childhood's mentors, although they never knew it. Those I admired were artists of sorts. Not necessarily painters or sculptors, but people who set up the conditions of life so that they could use their talents. I studied that finding like an unseen power. Discerning how best to live meant tracking down and cultivating my own "choosing-and-arranging skills," a phrase we'll explore shortly.

My mind seemed like a thought-train whizzing along unending tracks. I tried to watch receptively. That open looking increased over time. The more trust one had, the wider the view. Nonjudgmental observation altered things for the better.

In the garden that was childhood, didn't you also plant seeds for your life's purposes? Way back when, didn't you strive to master your mind and your emotions and try to decipher what had real meaning? Somehow I felt I was composing my life's story, being a faithful "chooser-and-arranger" of my own experience.

## Choosing-and-Arranging Artistry

Talent (and the desire to express it) orders and organizes the lives of highly creative, effective children. These children possess what John Briggs, writing about creatively gifted adults, terms "choosing and arranging skill": The ability to manage life according to an inner vision.[7] As with creative adults, by adolescence the spiritually intelligent youngster pulls away from elaborate family and social supports and shapes life so as to organize the gift.[8] Fear, low self-respect, self-consciousness, eagerness to belong, and certainly the "extreme situation" can cripple that artistry.

Despite being amply blessed with intellectual or environmental advantages, some high IQ children are just not very creative. Intellectual ability — a high IQ — is not precisely spiritual intelligence and certainly no guarantee of future achievement.[9] For example, when Louis Terman tracked a thousand high IQ people from childhood until they were well past middle age, he found that not a single "truly illustrious" person emerged.[10] Common experience clarifies the issue: When we *try* to gain popularity or approval or conform in order to avoid outright abuse, we generally plow our gifts underground, into disuse. Youngsters with high IQs may ignore their insights. Psychoanalyst Erich Fromm suggested that such self-betrayals occur in any child who habitually suppresses a truth:

> A five-year-old girl, for instance, may recognize the insincerity in her mother, either by subtly realizing that, while the mother is always talking of love and friendliness, she is actually cold and egotistical, or in a cruder way by noticing that her mother is having an affair with another man while constantly emphasizing her high moral standards. The child feels the

discrepancy. Her sense of justice and truth is hurt, and yet, being dependent on the mother who would not allow any kind of criticism and, let us say, having a weak father on whom she cannot rely, the child is forced to suppress her critical insight.[11]

If a conscious choice to ignore a parent's flaws or insincerity quickly becomes unconscious, then the youngster's ability to think and observe is undermined. Better to snuff out the valid but troublesome truth-teller within than to lose a parent's (or peer group's) love. According to Abraham Maslow, highly intelligent but noncreative children lose their "impulse voices": They look to parents, teachers, or other authority figures for their guidance and inspiration.[12] As we shall see in our next chapter, this outer-direction, particularly in the extreme, is the kiss of death to true joy.

John Briggs points out that a mark of creative genius is the individual's ability to choose and arrange the details of his or her expressive life according to some constant, forceful inner vision, shaping the life "to organize the gift."[13] Inspired youngsters choose-and-arrange the gestalt, or unified pattern, of their entire life. That seems integral to what I'm calling "early artistry," and the ability is propelled by

- an edifying, spiritual raison d'être,

- sturdy, workaday competencies,

- tenacity in executing plans.

Nowhere is this artistry more evident than in early awakeners who are in any way handicapped. They inspect and transmute every facet of their "dark" realities in the service of their light, and they demonstrate that artistry has two cooperating sides. I call both sides "self-sheltering": One side preserves the soul's aesthetic. It enables children to flourish. The other seems to be a survival reflex.

## Self-Sheltering Artistry

Let me explain: Subjective health is the good spiritual soil that nourishes early artistry. Emotionally healthy children are hungry to express their inner life truthfully, beautifully, in ways never seen before — regardless of how unattractive their circumstances may seem. All decent artists do this, too. The so-called obstacle of a small canvas or spilled black ink on clean, white paper becomes *useful*. The artist integrates seeming "mistakes" into fresh expressions. Mishaps and constraints force artists to tap into their nonconscious processes to express something new.

Before Helen Keller awoke to language and to love, she said she felt like a clod of earth, an animal seeking warmth and food.[14] Her gifts and her supposed limits urged her to tackle much somber business along with her joy. Keller studied her condition, yet denied it as a predicament in order to create and arrange her best options. Had she been overly compliant, self-conscious, a slave to circumstance, she might never have taken expressive strides. In effect, her artistry both sheltered her talents and let her survive.

We find a splendid example of early artistry in Ireland's best-selling novelist Christy Brown. Crippled in infancy by cerebral palsy, until age ten Brown didn't realize that his physical incapacities prevented a normal life.

He couldn't so much as wave to those he loved. But prior to a spurt of awareness, he played contentedly alongside his brothers, with only vague uneasiness that something about him was different. Discovery of his condition triggered a severe depression. Suddenly Brown's happy world crumbled:

> I couldn't reason this out. I couldn't even think clearly about it. I could only feel it, feel it deep down in the very core of me, like a thin sharp needle that worked its way through all the fancies and dreams of my childish mind till it tore them to shreds, leaving it naked and powerless to avoid the stark reality, that I was a cripple.[15]

Brown, like Keller, *studied* his situation — not precisely out of morbidity, but in order to live full out, to demonstrate his potential. Intent on becoming whole, he integrated his feelings, pulled them into sight, assimilated and used whatever was happening. That art protects talent. It also furthers survival. Creating and arranging a workable, self-expressive life depends on employing every jot and tittle of the present as means to something finer. "Self-sheltering" skill affirms hope. It presses inborn gifts into use. It preserves sanity. In other words, it renews — uncovers — the eternal values of our deepest humanity.

That integrative process seems to have initially drawn Brown into despair. He felt nothing could revive his old, cheery outlook. Yet, in the twinkling of an eye, love revealed a novel, unbounded opportunity. One Christmas morning, a box of rainbow paints and a soft, slender brush meant for, but rejected by, his brother came to Brown's attention. Instantly he knew he must, and would, possess these. Love led him "hot with excitement" to experiment with his left foot (the only part of his body over which he had control). First, he painted. Then he wrote. Then love inclined Brown (as it does each one who awakens) toward his vocation, his expressive, contributive future. Before that quickening, Brown felt life hardly worth living. Might not his description of that initial futility help us understand, in part, teenage depression, alcohol and drug use, and suicide? Could not his overcoming be learned by others? I believe we could alleviate much youthful despair simply by teaching boys and girls how to protect their inborn gifts. With our own stories, if nothing else, we might show youngsters that it is right and proper to develop the wholeness residing within.

In girlhood, one woman's family tried to bully her into abandoning her passion for art. By age five, insight beyond a mere high IQ led her to lock herself in her bedroom whenever she felt like painting. She said *love* (i.e., of painting) protected her from her family's meanness. I've written elsewhere about a community activist who told me that in boyhood he employed anger (e.g., fierce grimaces and clenched fists) to hold his toxic, seductive mother at arm's length. He hid in the family's sole bathroom to read "and take time out to think."

### Demonstrated Maturity

Spiritually precocious youngsters tend to embody the definition of emotional maturity provided by Dag Hammarskjöld, late United Nations secretary-general. He was, of course, describing a heroic type of atypical adult when he wrote that, among other thing, maturity means that we do not hide our strengths from fear and, consequently, choose to avoid our best.[16]

Early awakeners like Keller and Brown are, in most respects, simply children who, within the scope of their age or talents, refuse to live below their best. That's *demonstrated* maturity. We see it in boys and girls who wrestle or dance expertly or who face bullies or who exhibit exceptional valor as Eagle Scouts.

Benedictine monk Bede Griffiths wrote that in boyhood "no amount of noise" disturbed his reading. This is an everyday variety of demonstrated maturity. At night, Griffiths took books into the bathroom (the "only place where a light could be kept on with impunity") and read "with the book propped up against a board across the bath."[17]

Such acts signify not just age-appropriate initiative, not just a child's natural separation from the dictates of authority, but also the growth of fidelity — the quality Erik Erikson once defined as sustained loyalty to our chosen values in the face of conflicting values and expectations. A faithful individual is courageous, often advancing forward despite feeling the cold feet of fright. Maslow's notion of healthy autonomy is similar: Individuals learn to trust. Their creative contributions are strengthened vis-à-vis a wholesome independence. They are self-reliant but feel connected to others, not governed by dread or an inability to relate.

A sense of oneness with others produces these productive, faithful choices. If, as poets, monks, or inventors, we ultimately choose to work or live alone, we can do so knowing that our solitude enables us to passionately serve others, to share our gifts with them while being true to ourselves.

Compassionate adults can support children's healthy autonomy by talking with them about the importance of contributing to others. It is rarely enough to be told we are smart or have talent. By contrast, giving from an overflow of interior wealth is deeply fulfilling. To know that helps youngsters demonstrate their maturity.

## Power to Follow Love

In medieval times, some intensely spiritual boys and girls pleaded with their parents to send them to monasteries when they anticipated that their elders expected them to marry. This is similar to Theobaldus's pattern, but may not be identical. The uncommon child ran away from home to avoid what seemed to be a domestic enslavement. Ascetic youngsters generally knew, without being told, what spiritual disciplines their parents would oppose. So they meditated in their closets or fasted in secret. By age five, renowned mystic Catherine of Siena hid in the corners of her family home in order to pray. She could be heard reciting one Hail Mary for each step she took while climbing a long stairway.[18]

Teresa of Avila's religious ardor began during her earliest years. Around age five she pronounced herself willing to die for her faith. Soon after, she ran away to live as a hermit. Then she returned and lived in a cell in her family's garden as an example of tangible, demonstrated truth.[19]

To grow whole, all of us must choose between the expectations of significant, even beloved others and "the hidden, incorruptible man of the heart" (1 Pet. 3:4). Previously I proposed that in early awakeners the inner one overcomes externals, and all the more as the spiritual life unfolds. Not just traditional religious ardor but nature, art, and music, even grief or trauma can stimulate that unfolding. One young man (now a naturalist and a hospice volunteer) told me that in boyhood his spirituality was "underdeveloped or nonexistent." Both of his parents were active members of a large traditional church. Yet at home religion was never discussed:

> No one encouraged my unique spiritual experience. Throughout my childhood, my father seemed consumed with nervousness and anger. (His mom, my grandmother, was an evangelical type, which I suspect was a turn-off to him.) I have never discussed religion or spirituality with my father. He has always been a very emotionally distant man, rarely able to show love or affection toward his four kids.

During the family's yearly vacations in the High Sierra, the boy experienced nature's profundities:

> To return to one of your original questions, "Who, if anyone, in your family encouraged your distinctive spirituality?" the answer is *no one*. To a certain extent, I raised myself emotionally (more so as a teenager), and it was my time spent alone that led to the development of the relationship I have with myself. I had to be my own best friend.

## Conduct Demonstrates Maturity

Most young children find uncommon peace when they spend time in nature or listen to poetry or music or read. Some see, or feel, angelic beings guarding them. Others beg their parents to tell and retell them stories about saints, prophets, or family heroes and heroines. When they sense that their own fundamental goodness brings them to life, children search for examples of virtuous others who "share" their reality. Young, gifted leaders may favor tales about honesty and courage, or about characters who possess an innate power, shrewdness, fairness, or love of justice. By their fascination with the sacred, other-worldly aspects of death, religious youngsters might reflect their sense of God's presence in their everyday affairs. It's usual for children to show a healthy curiosity about the afterlife. In a similar vein, children with advanced math or musical ability fall in love with numbers or notes. These preoccupations can open the door to their life's artistry.

The acclaimed American artist Janet Scudder (1869–1940) was raised in grim surroundings. Her impoverished environment was bleak. That could have been a huge obstacle to Scudder's desire "to hitch her wagon to a star"[20] had the colors of her garden's flowers not stirred "something latent" in Scudder and released her creative gifts. At six years old, swept up by such "intense excitement" that she rushed indoors, Janet cried out to her blind grandmother: "I want to paint [flowers] like these. I've got to! I must!"[21] Scudder knew she was expected to become a teacher, like her sister. Instead, she followed love's summons. At her qualifying exams she willfully wrote "all the foolish answers" she could muster to the test, thus assuring the denial of a teacher's certificate.[22] Conduct demonstrates the child's distinctive love or spiritual maturity.

As a boy, Truman Capote began to write. He wrote late

into the night. If anyone asked him what he was doing, he answered that he was doing homework. By age seventeen, Capote was a polished, accomplished writer. For the religiously gifted, such as Teresa of Avila, running away may reveal a mature vocational choice. For visual artists, such as Janet Scudder, colors may stimulate a distinctive rebellion and give rise to authentic choices. For the verbally gifted such as Truman Capote, writing late into the night divulges life's probable path.

The fortunate ones find their way to a demonstrated maturity alone. Or they work with empathic, insightful counselors or psychoanalysts who help them move through confusion, guilt, or despair — for being odd or hurt or flawed — into the ebullience of some intrinsic truth. Whatever the age, as we transcend "adjustment," we express our authentic experience. We may begin therapy feeling resigned ("Well, hurt is just the way I have to be") or angry ("Look what they did to me"). Growth of spiritual maturity gradually lets us accept our (and others') humanity ("I see now that it's natural to feel some ambivalence about my father [or mother, family, friend, boss], and after all, it's sensible to recoil from those who abuse me, even if down deep I love them").[23] From the heart of increased compassion, demonstrated maturity eventually produces feelings of oneness, interconnectedness, acceptance of others and ourselves, awe for the entire cosmos.

## Sacrificial Disciplines

Spiritually precocious children may appear too glad or peaceable for our comfort. They give away their toys to neighborhood children, sharing too freely for our budget. One mother complained that her child accepted her father's routine mistreatment, adding,

> My daughter sees her dad's side. She's overly forgiving, unbiased, much too even-tempered. I worry that people will take advantage of her.

That selective asceticism could point to religious and spiritual gifts. When "sacrifice" or disobedience is motivated by ardor or extraordinary fair-mindedness, in otherwise wholesomely disposed children, it may be symptomatic of spiritual gifts — not problems.

It's known that gifted young leaders have a great interest in justice. They'll complain bitterly if a teacher plays favorites in class. Or they'll expect everyone at the dinner table to get an equal slice of an apple pie. If a virtue, such as love of justice or compassion, causes youngsters to consciously choose some self-sacrifice, it could mean a spiritual talent is unfolding.

Dorothy of Montau, a "representative saint" in the Middle Ages, strove from an early age to purify herself. She met with strenuous opposition — first from her family and later from her husband, who abused her. At six years of age she typically "subjected herself to various mortifications" and begged to undertake long fasts.[24] Her prayers were long, self-abnegating exercises. Dorothy prostrated herself for hours, moving about so strenuously that she perspired, even in winter.

If religious zeal of this sort discomforts us or seems a tad bizarre, consider the instinctive commitments of children who love to work with clay or collect butterflies: They, too, go overboard, willingly disciplining themselves to the strict standards and dictates of their art or science. It's said Isaac Newton believed he discovered gravity by thinking about it continually. I've heard that when naturalist Marlin Perkins (of television's *Wild Kingdom*) was young, he carried bugs and reptiles in every pocket. The story goes that in childhood, neighbors hesitated to shake hands with him, fearing that spiders and lizards would leap out from the boy's clothes. An artist remembered that while she was still a toddler, she located any pencil within reach and drew feverishly on everything, clean white walls included. Observing that, her parents made sure she had plenty of paper.[25] Different vocations call for different sacrifices. Furthermore, both productive and counterproductive purposes demand competency. For instance, as a basic, entry-level skill, leaders must attract followers. The greater the leader, the wider the constituency he or she must entice to share a vision of any sort.

In his teens, Malcolm X proved himself a gifted influencer (as do many young gang leaders). At age fourteen, passing for twenty-one, he worked on a train that ran between Boston and New York. During layovers he hung out in the Harlem bars. He admitted having entrepreneurial prowess on the streets. ("I kept turning over my profit, increasing my supplies, and I sold reefers like a wild man. I scarcely slept.")

In later years, Malcolm X wished he'd had a better academic education — studied law or linguistics, perhaps — "I would just like to *study,* because I have a wide-open mind."[26]

A high spiritual intelligence was percolating in Malcolm X's youthful consciousness. It bubbled up into awareness despite his life of teenage crime. Malcolm X was self-directed and charismatic. He influenced adults. He had drive, wit, and the same order of determination that led Capote to write late into the night and Bede Griffiths to read under the bedcovers and Scudder to flunk her teacher's exams in order to become a visual artist.

## Learning from Early Awakeners: Early Artistry

Early awakeners are acutely focused on what they love in ways that stimulate youthful commitments and activate

- needed self-discipline,
- the habits and routines by which to locate, then embody, their vocational universe,
- needed mechanical skills (such as expertise in playing the violin) and also healthy surrender to the sanctity of who one is.

The experience of awakening that cultivates such concentrated self-discipline also produces a profoundly spiritual oblation.

Even as babies, aware, sensitive children possess a sophisticated aesthetic intelligence. They may see beauty in numbers or stars or garden soil. Young visual artists appreciate subtlety of color or contrasting patterns of light more than other youngsters. I've heard professional dancers say they began twirling on their toes at two years old.

The word "spirituality" is derived from the Latin *spiritus,* or breath. *Spiritual* giftedness, per se, shows up through whatever breathes life into or enlivens a child's essential endowments and core self. That rule applies to us, no matter our age, cultural heritage, or belief system. We find this enlivening everywhere — in the famous, in the ordinary.

As a preschooler, Pulitzer Prize–winner Eudora Welty fell under the spell of stories. Her family nurtured her love of reading, hearing stories, and touching books:

> Regardless of where [books] came from, I cannot remember a time when I was not in love with them — with the books themselves, cover and binding and the paper they were printed on, with their smell and their weight and with their possession in my arms, captured and carried off to myself. Still illiterate, I was ready for them.[27]

A secretary told me that her son taught himself to read at age two. Like Welty, even as a toddler he felt intimately connected to books. Another parent watched her infant daughter (a musician today) repeatedly crawl up to the family piano, lift herself onto the bench so she could stand, and play the keys. The two-year old gurgled with delight when hearing her fingers make sounds. Infants' ears may be acutely attuned to selected tones: a bee's buzzing or notes from a guitar. As adults, such individuals usually remember their first encounter with insects or music. Often the initial meeting sparks life-long interest in a particular profession, as it did for a painter who reported that, even in his crib, the glosses and shades of color on his bedroom wallpaper mesmerized him: "As far back as I can recall, I have lived in space, not time.... My childhood memories [are coordinated] visually, not chronologically."[28]

As a child's religious gifts are expressed through love of the ineffable — virtue, prayer, God, the Bible — so diverse talents become apparent through other enjoyments that awaken children. We learn from early awakeners like Helen Keller or Christy Brown that when we follow ardor, the passion within our inherent gifts can move us "beyond IQ" into our own brand of artistry. That teaches us to shelter our talents, to discipline ourselves so we can use our gifts productively on behalf of self and other.

Fascination is another key to artistry, competence, and vocation. A particular engagement unleashes particular sorts of virtue, energy, and intelligence. That distinctiveness nurtured properly leads adults, at any age, to a functioning contributive love by which we actualize our place in the scheme of things. So much of this involves self-awareness. Artistry is linked to focus, fervor, and listening to the intrinsic whisper of our interior summons.

I'll wager no one *taught* you to lie down in sweet-scented grasses on sunny days and gaze up at blue skies, to watch the cloud-creatures floating by. Probably like any inspired child you taught yourself how to

- rearrange ideas,
- play with your building blocks of mind,
- visualize or imagine what you wanted.

Maybe as a child you experimented at night: before falling asleep, lying on cool, clean sheets in dark, hushed rooms, tucked under covers, breathing quietly, watching your thoughts. Did you concentrate on a line of prayer or a psalm — "He gives His angels charge over me, to guard me in all my ways" — to exchange forlorn images for ones that blessed you during sleep? Thoughts could be substituted, one for another, like pieces in an Erector set. That's artistry. Pure sport. Where did this lead? Straight to heaven, I for one imagined, as long as we plant our two feet squarely on the ground.

Moreover, *we're* not exactly discovering our "place," our competence, our vocation. We're *un*covering these. Place, competence, vocation — these are already ours, with us in consciousness since before the beginning.

# Chapter Eight

# Wholesome Autonomy

*I'm artistic. Both shy and outgoing. I'm mothering, self-reliant, and happy. I'd call myself an accepting, contented, and imaginative person. I'm also contemplative.* — Student, age thirteen

Christy Brown, on discovering that he could write by inserting a pencil between his first and second left toe, revealed what that meant to him:

> I wrote and wrote without pause, without consciousness of my surroundings hour after hour. I felt a different person. I wasn't unhappy anymore. I didn't feel frustrated or shut up anymore. I was free, I could think, I could create....
>
> ...I felt released, at peace. I could be myself sometimes anyway. And if I couldn't know the joy of dancing I could know the ecstasy of creating.[1]

To endure all manner of hardships, from the frustration of some physical limit, to rigorous study, to constant feelings of alienation for being different, a child must locate the mind's door to freedom: the imagination. This door opens up the artistry discussed in the last chapter. All artistry — whether it protects talent or life itself — leans

134

on that learning which cultivates autonomy (independence). How can any of us develop the power to envision what the metaphysician Neville called "better than the best we know" if, in our mind, we identify with corrupted images? Through fantasy play, reading, the study of math, science, or art, the child's imagination reveals a wide and boundless cosmos. Both hardship and joy can stimulate imagination, and the spiritually intelligent use their imagination like artists use paints and brush.

Some children consciously exploit the sheer gladness of their ideas or probe difficulties for a peek at future freedoms. Invention gushed from the inspired Antoine de Saint-Exupéry "like a boiling spring." In boyhood when he shared his drawings of flying with other children, he exclaimed,

> And when I shall fly away on my new machine, the entire crowd will cry: "Long live Antoine de Saint-Exupéry."[2]

Other children use their upsets imaginatively, simply to survive. They find strengths and purposes as they press through their disturbances. It's as if each child *requires* exercise for the imagination, at least a couple of lusty battles to build the warrior skills needed to master life. If I understand Howard Gruber's principle, as individuals solve problems they construct a point of view toward which they are inherently moving.[3] Youngsters are no different.

The autobiography of pioneering anthropologist Margaret Mead sheds light on one type of supportive home environment that supports independent learning. Margaret was reared in a climate that encouraged autonomous thought. The adults around her were bright and curious. Her mother and grandmother used cultural pursuits to reinforce her formal education.[4] Her paternal grandmother is said to have been an inspired tutor. She taught Margaret how to keep daily, anecdotal records on the infant development of her two younger sisters. Mead credits both her mother and grandmother for helping her see that "the mind is not sex-typed." Mead's early learning motifs suggest that a young person's inherent passion for some field can come to life by judicious, intimate encouragement:

> Throughout my childhood [my grandmother] talked a great deal about teachers, about their problems and conflicts and about those teachers who could never close the schoolhouse door behind them.... Grandma always wanted to understand things, and she was willing to listen or read until she did.... [She] set me to work taking notes on [my sister's] behavior — on the first words Priscilla spoke and on the way one echoed the other. She made me aware of how Priscilla mimicked the epithets and shouts hurled up and down the back stairs by the Swedish nurse and the Irish cook and of how Elizabeth was already making poetry of life.[5]

Spiritual intelligence may fill youngsters with awe for their gifts or for a heartfelt vocation. However, neither gifts nor awe automatically crown anyone as a master of fate. Competence, ability to concentrate, self-discipline, and a cultivated intuition of what supports growth and the point of view all help children voice whatever needs saying. The groundwork for every sort of spiritual advancement begins in childhood — as whole-some autonomy is established.

## Overview: Wholesome Autonomy

Lifelong interests and vigorous intellectual autonomy are cultivated in children whose imaginative gifts are challenged. When a demand is placed on inspired young-sters, they'll want to dig deep within to develop hidden potentials. By contrast, children who are subjected to con-tinuing threats — as in "the extreme situation" — tend to lose power. Fromm's constellation of traits for adults he called "productive types" includes the ability to

- use one's powers,
- realize one's inherent potentialities,
- remain unmasked, transparent, nonalienated, and real.

Fortunately, it doesn't take an idyllic, blemish-free homelife to cultivate wholesome autonomy. The great majority of those high-achieving ("eminent") children studied by Victor and Mildred Goertzel came from homes with an obvious love of learning: "Fewer than 10 per cent of the parents failed to show a strong love of learning . . . and children enjoyed being tutored, whether by professional tutors or by their parents."[6]

However, the Goertzels found a large number of cre-ative, eminent adults grew up in chaotic circumstances. They were active, enthused learners. Many had tutors, typically enjoyed studying, and even *needed* frequent, ongoing contact with bright, caring adults.[7] These find-ings reinforce earlier points about play. All inquisitive preschoolers require "play." It is their occupation. Play structures a child's explorations, work ethic, resource-fulness, and, hopefully, his or her adroit, cooperative interpersonal life. When a teacher responds to these needs, providing individualized, democratic, and respect-ful treatment, rebellion decreases. As proposed all along, wholesome spiritual attributes develop when a young-ster's inner life is dignified.

## Early Education and Healthy Autonomy

Today's home-schooling trends may foster that dignity: Parents as teachers can be excellent tutors — like Mead's family, attentive and curious. Modern home-schoolers, an estimated 500,000 to 1 million in the U.S., tend to perform well on standardized tests. Parent-teachers have new support: Internet chat rooms, proliferating web-site resources, and specialized sports leagues are all read-ily available. Furthermore, when they are responsive to the child, private home-tutors tend not to provoke the "venom" which public school teachers so often do.[8] Children who *feel* dignified treat others with reciprocal dignity, and all reasonably decent teachers convey that esteem, without fawning.

Bruno Bettelheim, who studied the effects of the origi-nal kibbutz on the emerging stabilities and competencies of kibbutz-raised adults, concluded that while each infant needs a "center," "a star by which to navigate," that star need not be the mother so long as "repeated, definite di-rections are provided" as to how the child is expected to behave. Some initial advantages for children raised in the early climate of the pre-1970s kibbutz appear to be:

- ample gratification of physical and other instinctual needs,

- little pressure to control those needs in the early years,

- optimal conditions for independence in childhood, and

- plenty of immediate attention (that furthers active exercise of self-initiatives).[9]

Montessori classrooms provide a different form of education yet include much the same ingredients as the kibbutz: Although children live at home, they have ample freedom of choice. Montessori teachers organize both play and learning. To Maria Montessori, *work* was that "life-in-process," or progressive actualizing, that teachers can enhance in every child.[10] Whether in a kibbutz, a home-school, or a Montessori classroom, attitudes that cultivate an enduring love of learning promote self-acceptance and lack of alienation.

## Personal Patterns

My own early education involved "home-schooling" and was much like a communal set-up — as in a kibbutz or a Montessori system. I grew up in a time and place when parents of a certain social set hired governesses and private teachers to raise their children. It was years before I realized not every girl had her own live-in tutor. My governess, Madame P., a former Russian aristocrat, had lost everything — husband, home, social standing, wealth — in some political uprising. I never got her story straight and can't say whether she'd had children. Refined austerity and an iron will helped Madame P. weather her storms of financial and family destitution. She is immortalized in my memory as a true master of forbearance. While my grandmother encouraged my spiritual interests, Madame P. demonstrated what one person could accomplish by blending private strategies with a fierce determination to survive.

As gentle and soft-spoken as my mother, as intrepid as any general, Madame P. mandated a military-like regimen. A structured routine, which I loved, fostered in me a modicum of self-control and a watery, tentative confidence — two traits I sorely needed to alleviate my anxiety and handle the weirdness around me. Learning the basics, reading and language arts, at the daybreak of youth didn't hurt either, since a love of learning and an ability to express oneself benefit anyone's life. Learning and a sort of cultural mastery were highly prized, and rewarded, in our home.

### Day-to-Day Learnings

Each morning at first light, Madame P. woke me for our long dawn constitutional. Rain or shine, we two covered miles of dirt road. We conversed only sporadically to insure a brisk walk and plenty of fresh air. After that came breakfast. Mine consisted of hot porridge and steamy goat's milk (with a disgusting skin floating on top). Next came reading lessons. From about age three on, I read voraciously in both English and Russian, spoke the two languages fluently, and understood French — my parents' native tongue. (Once Madame P. left my side, my affinity for foreign languages vanished.) Daily study continued until lunch, after which I napped. Then I was free to do whatever I chose until tea-time, at about four o'clock. Occasionally, my mother and grandmother joined us, in which case within that well-bred circle of dainty tea-sippers sat agreeably one jolly little girl, feeling very grown up and loving that theater of high civility.

When her friends visited, my mother paraded me about like a wind-up doll. I was supposed to read aloud or re-cite short Russian verses to impress everyone with my tricks. I soon tired of the limelight and stubbornly re-fused to entertain, especially if I had to dress up or hug the multitudes.

## Learning the Basics

Madame P. educated and supervised my day-to-day comportment. Although the constellation of grown-ups around me was thoroughly diverse, early childhood found me swimming in a sea of homogeneous values. More-over, I cannot imagine integrating into one's life such ephemeral values as courtesy, cooperation, kindness, or industriousness unless people we love and admire (who love and admire us) convey those qualities through their own behavior. *That's* character development.

Everyone significant to me had an indefatigable respect for honesty, for learning (but not necessarily formal ed-ucation), and for social refinement. I rarely heard the grown-ups raise their voices, and I was not supposed to raise mine or be rude in any way (although I was). Ours wasn't a rigid household. Just extraordinarily polite.

In all this, Madame P. was a kind, if exacting, coach.

For her, "control" never meant "controlling." A remarkably progressive educator, Madame P. had no formal training. Her teaching methods were strict and firm: Lessons began and ended punctually. We covered the ground we set out to cover and trekked tediously, meticulously, through the basics. The *content* of my studies, however, was rich and flexible. Here my curiosity ruled. There was little — art, literature, my pets, the war, our games, all the stuff of daily life — that Madame P. (or my family, for that matter) did not exploit as educational fodder. The point is that I was taught that learning and healthy independence are inextricably linked.

## Learning for Self-Mastery

The child who actively employs her mind eventually sees she can use it for self-mastery. Even inspired children can feel afraid of confronting a jealous sibling or rejecting a manipulative adult. To manage trouble, they'll learn to trust their gut, take risks, be single-minded. To survive small skirmishes and eventually larger ones, a certain doggedness is required.

In the sanctity of their own hearts, children decide what to protest or go along with. Saying no is not a gamble. Skills are involved in risk-taking — mixed variables to assess, for example, how one feels versus what one thinks. Even a child waits for the just right moment to ask for a larger allowance or permission to try something new. A recent college graduate told me that in elementary school letter writing solved a communication problem. She and her mother had trouble discussing things. They exchanged notes as a substitute for talking. Their written dialogue

flowed out of need. It saved time and preserved trust between the two. When mother and daughter argued, one
slipped under the other's door a letter of explanation or
a loving apology. Currently an English major with a flair
for poetry, the young woman fondly recollects how they
"conversed" when speaking didn't work:

> We wrote to each other until I was sixteen. Writing
> is now for me a freeing expression. The creative side
> of that came from my mother. Birthdays, Valentine's
> Day and holidays brought all of us notes from her.
> My dad wrote to us too, and I wrote to connect with
> them both. As a family, we're all still really close —
> much more so than my friends seem to be with their
> parents.

That family's interpersonal patterns enhanced everyone's closeness. In these nurturing, personalized settings
a child can be inquisitive. He or she learns that there is
a synergy between solving problems and joy — even im-
proved relationships. Positive gratification, not threats or
pressure to measure up, is the best motivator for wholesome autonomy. The youngster learns, "It's possible for
me to think things through and contribute to the smooth
running of things."

We return to this theme, what educator Herbert Kohl
terms "assent in learning," in the next chapter on early
rebellion. *Not* learning is often a wholesome form of
protest and a developing autonomy that pursues self-
knowledge — the discovery of who one is, what is valued,
what one loves, wants, and ought to do. Maslow once
wrote that optimal learning is a value quest that circles
the "ought questions" such as, "What ought I to do?"

A child's wholesome independence is boosted when empathic adults limit unsolicited advice ("You should do thus or such") and help a child investigate options, explore feelings, and listen inwardly in lifelong exploration of "ought questions" such as

- What ought I to be?
- How can I best solve this conflict?
- Should I pursue this career or that one?
- Ought I choose this way or that?
- Should I live or die?[11]

By contrast, some parents are pathetically inept teachers. You'd never find them writing notes to a child. Even if their child is socially adroit, the adults cannot — or won't — reciprocate. I've met parents and teachers who are a few beats short of getting what anyone is saying. While such adults also lack teaching skills and a mature discernment, it's their overall dullness — their apathy, confusion, or hostility — that exacerbates even the small, totally predictable problems of growing up. Over time, healthy, spiritually intelligent children back away. They stop communicating. For sensitive youngsters, a *little* scolding goes a long way, and all extreme punishment can ruin childhood. It's as if some adults are deficient in feeling for the tender heart of a child.

## The "Early Pledge" for Self-Mastery

We find an example of that tenderness as well as that "backing away" in a vignette from the life of Live-Aid organizer Bob Geldof. After his mother died and until adolescence Geldof excelled in his studies at a Belfast parochial school. At that point, his need for pocket change drove him to pilfer money from his own tuition fund. According to Geldof, when the school's priests and Geldof's father discovered the offense they colluded on his "just rewards," agreeing that the boy deserved severe beatings to learn that stealing was a sin. The headmaster-priest summoned young Geldof to his office, branding him a liar and a sinner, whipped him with a "thick, flexible rubber strap [that] hurt unbearably,"[12] and sent him home alone, in pain and in terror of the prospect of yet another beating. Geldof found his father waiting to thrash him. The man coldly revealed his intent to hit his son six times with a bamboo cane. Pleading for mercy proved useless ("I still didn't really grasp what had been so bad"). The beating commenced. Geldof ran from the first searing blows. Father chased son around the dining room and finished the job, after which he sought to make amends. Geldof's comments illustrate the workings of a spiritual intelligence that grasps hypocrisy in any disguise:

> At the end, the bastard tried to hug me. How dare he salve his own pathetic conscience with that act of hypocrisy? If you're going to hurt someone, hurt them, but don't pretend it's love. That's perversion. I was filled with disgust and I hated him. The hurt, the rage, the shame and the bewilderment were too deep. From that day on, my father and I were at loggerheads. He would pay.
>
> This was not a conscious decision, more an unconscious *understanding*. There was no one I could talk to, no one to go home to, so *forced in on myself*

*I became self-sustaining and self-reliant.* (emphasis added)[13]

Geldof's boyhood vow to trust only himself flowed from a vivid, defining learning experience. Adult insensitivity, unfairness, and phoniness apparently triggered the youngster's loyalty — to himself. He registered his pain. He felt the injustice. He planned corrective actions and executed them accordingly. Geldof's unwillingness to feign admiration for either his father or the school priests seems to me a mark of inspiration — the life force or "I Am" with us all that will not be denied nor dishonored.

That story reminds me of a caller on a radio show who told me that he believed he is successful today because in boyhood he assured himself he would always tell himself the truth: "I've lied to others, but I've kept my word of honor to myself." Our innate wisdom commands loyalty to that "I Am" by refusing to let us

- cooperate with inhuman systems,
- accept counterfeit love,
- grant control or power to abusers.

Geldof's wholesome independence must have taken giant strides the day he pledged to become "self-sustaining and self-reliant." If we give ourselves our solemn word that we will not ignore the brutes in our midst, we liberate ourselves.

Consider an opposite scenario, where from infancy through late childhood a child is deprived of adult understanding or protection. As noted, Geldof had known and felt a loving mother at his side. Suppose she had died earlier. Suppose a child is passed around to relatives or to a series of foster homes. Imagine if the preschool years do not offer a boy or girl a reliable, loving haven that nature intends early childhood to be. Under those conditions, if "the extreme condition" exists, the traits of wholesome autonomy might never be properly assimilated. In that eventuality, rebellion could be negative, by which I mean independence of thought and deed would turn against self and others. As Freud, Fromm, Erikson, Maslow, and others stress, if we don't learn to love and work productively, wholeness gets warped.

We can assess such possibilities using a story about the preschool years of the novelist, creative genius, and samurai Mishima. Mishima was born in 1925 to a middle-class couple living in Japan. Biographer John Nathan recounts that, at forty-nine days old, the infant was named Kimitake. The next day — at age fifty *days* — his paternal grandmother, Natsu, took the infant away from his mother. Natsu appears to have tyrannized the entire household. When Natsu removed the baby from his mother, she

> moved him, crib and all, to her darkened sick-room downstairs. And there she held him prisoner until he was twelve, jealously, fiercely, hysterically guarding him against his parents and the outside world.... Certainly her insane possessiveness suggests that her motives were largely selfish; it was as if she wanted someone to share the burden of her physical pain... her comprehensive despair.[14]

Kimitake's father and mother soon separated. Overly protected by his grandmother during all his years with her, the child had no real grasp of how to function. He was "sick," "frail," teased at school, and called a runt. Natsu arranged it so that he could miss his physical education classes. She restricted his diet to a bland, monotonous fare (so that he wasn't able to eat in the cafeteria with the other children), and "until he was in the fourth grade" she would not let him go on school outings.

When Kimitake was nine years old, the family moved to a compound with two houses. There he lived with the infirm grandmother and was made to minister to her night and day. He lived and slept in her room. He had to "sponge her brow and massage her back and hip; and it was Kimitake who led her by the hand on her frequent trips to the toilet. The worst times were at night."[15] The boy stared at the ceiling unable to sleep, listening to Natsu's groans. She cried "like one possessed." While growing up, he met with many other piercing cruelties. He rarely complained.

By age sixteen, Kimitake was a prolific but tortured genius. He became known as Mishima, one of Japan's premier authors:

> He had written forty novels, eighteen plays (all lavishly performed), twenty volumes of short stories, and as many of literary essays. He was a director, an actor, an accomplished swordsman and a muscle man ... had been up in an F-102 and had conducted a symphony orchestra; seven times he had traveled around the world, three times he had been nominated for the Nobel Prize ... [and] was besides, an international celebrity. . . . [16]

Despite worldly success, at age forty-six Kimitake took his own life in a ritual protest related to classical Japanese values of honor and a samurai ethic. He committed hara-kiri, *seppuku,* in a large public square.

It is not precisely Mishima's final act but his lifelong despair and overall worldview that warrant comment. He admits in letters to friends, written at about age sixteen, that he's "unwholesome," that he's made a masquerade of normalcy and is alienated. He feels contempt for many universal values, like peace, which Kimitake calls "tedious" and "insipid." In the closing lines of one essay he "gets down to what he really misses: 'Running blood..., the gushing river of blood.'"[17] Shortly before his suicide, which he planned carefully for at least a year, Mishima confided to his mother that he had "never done anything in his life that he had wanted to." In adulthood he meditated on the desirability of death, saying that he longed for death in adolescence and that he tasted a

> special excitement...as he watched Tokyo burn in 1945 [at the end of World War II, sensing] the fiery apocalypse near at hand. He wonders how to recapture that excitement.[18]

Mishima's is an extreme illustration that antilife is learnable too.

Contrast Mishima's self- and worldview with that of artist, philosopher, and social activist Ben Shahn. Shahn grew up in a religious, somewhat strict Jewish home. He was loved and respected. Expectations for him were set high; adult-like standards were applied. His mother and father spoke of distant European relatives with great affection. Ben's far-off family, as well as venerable figures in Scripture, were integrated in his psyche as kindred spirits. He felt an early private goal: "to learn to draw — and to learn to draw always better and better." His family encouraged his instinctive love of art. Shahn was required to study hard. He learned a craft and contributed in a qualitatively superior fashion to his community. One senses that his childhood was a focused adventure in unitive learning, an interval of years designed to shepherd Ben into right relationship with himself and others and that his shimmering universe of enchantment was destined to be expressed in sacred trust.

Elementary school involved nine hours of classroom attendance each day. After that Shahn had chores to do. At age fourteen, he was apprenticed to a lithographer. Thus, years before graduation he had studied the Bible, ingested prayers and the psalms ("my first music, my first memorized verse"), learned about type and lettering, and embraced people, both living and dead, as an intimate, integral aspect of his boyhood world. "Other" was self.

Unlike Mishima, Shahn did not continually need to protect himself against toxic intrusions. Rather, like a flower lifts its face to the sun, Ben turned toward life, service, and authentic caring, expected to share of himself through bountiful, functional excellence. Life was to be sanctified with all one's wit and strength. In one remarkable autobiographical passage, we sense Shahn's psyche:

> All the events of the Bible were, relatively, part of the present. Abraham, Isaac and Jacob were "our" parents — certainly my mother's and father's, my grandmother's and my grandfather's, but mine as well.
>
> I had no sense of imminent time and time's passing such as was felt and expressed by my own daughter.

...All the secure and settled things were not settled at all.... Time was moving toward me, and time
was passing away. It seemed as though there wasn't
enough of it for anyone.[19]

## Learning from Early Awakeners: Wholesome Autonomy

The more love dominates the mind and learnings of a
child, the more wholesome independence grows. That's
additive, a progression, a gaining of spiritual qualities
we recognize as virtue, self-sacrifice, sharing, asceticism,
and sober thought. Children who are encouraged (even
if strictly disciplined) to develop their unique gifts and
perspectives attend to their own interests (rather than
someone else's). As we see in Shahn, that's how they serve.
Doing so, they give what's substantive; they serve in a
fashion that unfolds who, genuinely, they are. Precursors
of that healthy trajectory include

- developing an active, fruitful imagination,
- using both joy and difficulty to shape an enduring, life-affirming point of view,
- facing appropriate challenges that cultivate love of the continual learning that resourcefully discerns what's needed here and now.

If we haven't been raised in an intellectually open
atmosphere, it's likely we can find time and sufficient freedom in adulthood to arrange that climate for ourselves.
The first step is to stabilize ourselves in the love at our
ground of being. A youngster like Bob Geldof, beaten
and degraded by the chief authority figures in his life, can

grow up to serve life if his inner experience is shielded or somehow healed.

It's the too-obedient child we should worry about, the one whose delicate feeling-life and intuition get smashed. If we believe we must kowtow to those who dash our finest aspirations, then we should get ourselves to a healer, fast. Wholesome independence requires a sturdy sense of self. For that, we need to

- develop the degree of self-trust and respect required to project our finest experience of reality into the world,

- love and work productively and in our distinctive way,

- solve problems so that in the long run, if not sooner, everyone wins,

- locate meaningful, superordinate purposes that continually affirm life.

Geldof decided alone and with feisty license how to handle his home situation. He found courage to leave home, to never look back. That same split-second vow is reported by many other adults with a pit-bull's determination to transcend something potentially damaging. When those vows are rooted in love of life, it is the start of healthy autonomy. Only a start.

Wholesome independence fuels our determination to survive and flourish. It must become a productive fire in the belly. Otherwise our intensity, creative drive, and dynamism can turn inward, producing spirit*less* ends. However hard we fight against something (an enemy, an abuser, a punitive policy), healthy autonomy requires

- productive, boundary-setting choices,
- constructive choices (not simply originality or striking out),
- learning what's of value and independently expressing some whole ideal,
- reconciliations with painful learning experiences.

Everything discussed is linked, dove-tailed, all-of-a-piece, and whole:

- inspired thought,
- interior authority,
- artistry,
- the truth that leads to a fruitful independence,
- meaningful purposes.[20]

So where was St. Theobaldus when I needed him? He wiped out objections to his spiritual liberty with a single, fluid utterance. Theobaldus was nippy — or I should say well seasoned. His speech was salted with authority. There was flavor to what he said. People listened. And rightly so, for "salt is good: but if the salt has lost its saltiness, wherewith will ye season it? Have salt in yourselves, and have peace with one another" (Mark 9:50, KJV).

I was not so fully enlivened. As a child, I knew (and was quick to be reminded) that one is expected to love one's parents (which I did), that virtuous children are obedient (which, ordinarily, I was), and that when accommodating their parents' whims, "good" children defer to authority to an ingratiating extreme. That I could never do. True, my bid for independence was active and strategic, but it was largely cerebral. It took me years to wrest free of a double-minded, mealy-mouthed propriety. Thomas Merton gives us spiritual direction for correcting that: "In manifesting our inmost aspirations...we should strive above all to be frank and clear."[21]

St. Theobaldus could "honor father and mother" only when he honored God. We learn from that story that the press of frankness and a superordinate vocation comes from within. Young Theobaldus instructs us plainly: Wholesome independence follows a sacred love that is "no respecter of persons." We heed love, as I mean the phrase, only by

> the practice of a form of attention which is rare in itself and impossible except in solitude; and not only physical but mental solitude. This is never achieved by [one] who thinks of himself as a member of a collectivity, as part of something, which says "We."[22]

I can almost hear some readers murmuring, "A summary such as you've offered is well and good, but *how* do we cultivate the critical ephemerals — self-respect and increased, universal love?" To answer, I share one more tidbit of sagacious Ben Shahn advice that I copied on an index card, stuck on a cork-board above my workspace, and have thought about nearly every day since encountering it around 1975. In the following passage, Shahn addresses artists about fellow painter Paul Klee. Yet his message encourages anyone. He says every one of us, even if we have nothing else — "not even an Eames chair" — has this one thing:

> a wholly separate and individual self, with his own dreams and passions, its unique landscape un-

mapped and unexplored — peopled with shapes and forms unknown to others. And that private, unknown self, wherever it has been realized well, in paint, sculpture, music or words, has been of unceasing value and wonder to others.[23]

Whoever experiences the integrity of his or her inner landscape cannot help but grow toward wholesome autonomy. For some, therapy introduces that private self. For others, spiritual direction, a Bible study group, or talks with a trusted friend provide means for interior exploration. For yet others, a loving marriage, the birth of a child, or the death of a loved one prompts the venture. Prayer and meditation are my most viable routes to the still point of Self.

As I considered my delayed response to early disquiet, one day the idea sprang forth, full blown: The growing unrest, violence, or seeming undoing of our culture can only be healed by spiritual means. Healing, collective or individual, is no cerebral affair. Our existential insights about joy, hurts, or moral dilemmas surface as we enter what philosopher Max Picard called the Presence that is our still point. In that optimal communion we're not debating or theorizing *about* the Spirit. We are intimately at-one with self-originating Love, and as we read in Psalm 147, that union is what "healeth the broken in heart and bindeth up their wounds."

At any age, resting faithfully beneath pain or surface appearances, we meet our own integrity unfolding, from its core. To reword an old Japanese proverb, once that integrity is liberated, wild-horses cannot stop its assertions that our joy may be fulfilled.

# Chapter Nine

# Positive Rebellion

*I'm a troublemaker. They say I talk too much. To this point, what's influenced me are the beatings I've had.*
— Student, age fourteen

As a young girl Catherine of Siena cut off all her hair to avoid an arranged marriage. She then accepted her punishment as if it were a form of religious asceticism, using it to discipline and purify herself. In Catherine, we note one verity of healthy protest: For better or worse, young rebels are generally livelier than their more passive counterparts. Some inner reality forbids such children to budge from their authentic purposes or blindly succumb to the rule of authority.

Positive rebellion like Catherine's can be perplexing. Adults rightly expect reasonable compliance from the young. Appropriate courtesy and cooperation further the youngster's well-being and instill among other things the self-disciplines needed to get ahead, to learn, and to be productive. Ultimately, no one advances in life who doesn't get along with others. Friendships, we now hear, can prolong life. It's also commonly accepted that much youthful rebellion is simply an immature reactiveness. Knee-jerk protests can undermine fruitful study, commitments, or relationships.

On the other hand, it is the norm for the spiritually intelligent to protest when sheltering their gifts or pioneering some line of thought. (We saw in the last chapter that unwholesome protests turn against life.) Sensitive, self-referring children speak up, but not always constructively. Sometimes they defy adults. They rebel, not only *against* rules and authority, per se, but also *for* themselves.

In childhood, spiritual intelligence stirs the readiness to demonstrate — or act out — integrity. Readiness counts for so much. To understand the positive, self-sheltering principle is to accept that the truth seeking expression in a child is the same truth that's in us, the reality that glorifies our Lord and makes God say, "I have no greater joy than that my children walk in truth" (3 John 4).

## Overview: Positive Rebellion

Positive rebellion flows from an instinctive impulse to protect some seminal spiritual integrity. A child's choosing-and-arranging acts can shape the constructive conditions required to nurture an entire life's work. There are too many forms of productive protest to list. Each flows out of a distinctive psyche and environment. In general, signs of healthy, youthful protest may encompass what at first glance seem counterproductive acts, including

- a decision to fail,
- the defying of adults,
- not-learning.

Rebellion could be (and usually is) as uncomplicated as a student preferring to sit quietly under a tree and read

*Anne of Green Gables* while other children chase about playing soccer.

Positive rebels have an advantage over their more docile counterparts. Forthrightness saves time. It releases creative energy. It airs out emotions. Purposefulness and the stubborn desire to flourish fuel a justified assertion.

It is recognized that assertive youngsters tend to receive more attention and help at school than the subdued. The assertive are more likely to fend off bullies and molesters and less likely than passive children to attract sexual abuse. Molesters seek out the "quiet, withdrawn, compliant, easier to manipulate" boy or girl, the ones who are unlikely to "put up a fight."[1] Feelings of rage, frustration, fear, or depression get vented through emphatic words and choices. As suggested, self-affirming choices give children the strength to defend a *life*-affirming reality. But sturdy self-authority and a tenacity for coping during traumatic times are gained at a price.

In her superb discussion of childhood dissent, psychoanalyst Dr. Alice Miller recounts with pathos the punishment meted out to German novelist Hermann Hesse in his boyhood for daring to defy his mother. To control her son's rebellion, Hermann's mother banished him to an institution for epileptics and "defectives." The family conditioned the boy's release on his "improvement." He did rehabilitate himself and did return home. But not before revealing his true feelings.

Prior to what Miller calls his "restoration of denial and idealization of his parents," he censured both parents by telling them that only if he were a bigot and not a human being could he hope for their understanding.[2] Hermann's confrontative honesty illustrates the kind of rebellion I call "positive": It affirms life, the truth of one's being. It upholds something valued. It has a deeply spiritual logic. Hermann knew the truth and spoke it. That assertion is a condition of sound mental health, although grave consequences may follow. Demonstrated maturity calculates the risk.

Hesse's youthful predicament sheds light on the plight of sensitive children who are mistreated or manipulated away from feeling safe and away from their finest perceptions. It doesn't take a genius to break a child's spirit. No kindness or wisdom at all is required to drive children wild with fear or drive underground their perceptiveness and bury (or, as in Hesse's case, delay) further truth-telling. With active, empathic listening and cooperative dialogue, adults can help children apply their powers of protest intelligently. Barring that nurturance, young people learn how to object on their own. But we adults may not like the outcomes of the latter.

Miller is emphatic: What disturbs us is not our early family traumas, but the falsehoods and mixed messages that confuse us; these our innocence finds tough to untie. Especially crushing are what she calls, "the absurdities of our own mothers" when, as helpless children, we were most in need of mature, selfless love and did not get it. To become self-respecting adults, children must become consciously attuned to their parents' "unconscious manipulations and their unintended narcissisms."[3] Full-blown wholeness requires us to

- consciously liberate ourselves from false guilt,

- reject artificial obligations,

- overcome self-condemnation for cowardice and narcissism in childhood,
- divorce our self-involved, hurtful elders: parents, subverting influencers, and the like.

Miller adds that only then can we mourn our losses, forgive, and move on.

Psychiatrist Robert Lindner proposed that almost all of us are seduced by a swan song of conformity whose refrain is "You must adjust."[4] Our instinct for rebellion is an invaluable trait of our humanity. Sadly, many adults discourage even the most constructive assertions of youth. They promote a timeless tension between authentic individuals and society. Child-rearing biases, or perhaps ego, get in the way. I have seen teachers misunderstand or, worse, ride roughshod over students. Most elementary-age youngsters would not launch their "acting out" strategies were it not for the bullying on some adult's part. So-called character development is often despotic.

## Personal Patterns

All things being equal, I adored pleasing both of my parents and never managed much mischief — except in school, I'll grant you that. In class one morning, before my father died, when things at home were bleak and my creative juices and frustration were bubbling over, my teacher announced that she did not wish our class to watch *I Love Lucy*. In her opinion, *Lucy* was televised much too late.

She told us that she had advised all the parents that it would be prudent to turn off the television early, to give us children a long night's sleep. That decision, I fumed, was none of her business, and her letter violated our constitutional rights. (I'm not so sure it did.) Preoccupied as they were, my parents never would have read her missive had I not set out to play class advocate. A petition seemed a deft touch. Mine declared that, from this day forth we, the undersigned, expected the school to mind its own affairs. Astonishingly, nearly the entire seventh grade endorsed the petition after I had etched my name conspicuously on the first dotted line. Questionable wisdom.

My father was summoned by the principal to fetch me from school, and he was livid. When he arrived, he refused to look at me and drove me home in Arctic silence. Later when he'd calmed down, he gruffly inquired if I had considered the gravity of signing and circulating petitions. Instantly, I knew my act had evoked sobering memories for my father: images of war-time confinement, powerless years spent in what I only assume was fear and squalor, in a perilous political setting where trivial dissent brought grotesque consequences. I did not regret my petition antic, but felt remorse for causing my father any pain. I never meant to upset him.

On the basis of that and other similar episodes, it's fair to say that after we arrived in the United States, I began to understand my father. He was, I came to see, a man who preferred a demure, mild-mannered daughter, someone more like her mother, a "little lady" who kept her assertions under the wrap of fetching, self-effacing appearances. That was news to me. Wasn't he the one who so outspokenly admired the courage of people like Eleanor Roosevelt? And taught me about deciphering the truths of my own heart? From my perspective, I'd been raised to think for myself, to root for underdogs, and to be outspoken. And anyway that's what I enjoyed. Furthermore, what he had in mind was abhorrent. I'd seen first hand what undue compliance got you: a tormented mind. I felt that a minimal level of adroit aggression (i.e., sometimes a bit more than just polite assertion) is required to outgrow childishness and move into a full-out contributive life. Paraphrasing scholar and novelist Dorothy L. Sayers, I did not wish to simply be pleasing; I wanted to enjoy myself as a complete human being.

## Self-Sheltering Rebellion vs. Self-Punishing Compliance

Outspokenness is no cut-and-dried affair. Countless intangibles intersect, to achieve or truncate a protest's constructive outcomes: timing, sound judgment, the stability and habitual response of all the players, the atmosphere and culture surrounding youthful assertion, the issues being rebelled against. Numerous elements coalesce to render a rebellious act "negative" or "positive." Earlier I called self-sheltering a requirement of artistry. Children develop that skill as they choose-and-arrange their circumstances according to their vision of possibilities. A creative child like Kimitake may be taught from infancy that his true self must bow to the collective. In fact, his individual integrity, the true self, is more critical to well-being than any societal influence. An intuitive realization of that fact often drives children's disobedience and emotional upheavals. Few children have the verbal skill to articulate their feelings. For that matter, most adults fall short of the mark, too.

In a poignant short story describing such self-sheltering intangibles, poet and educator Sandra Cisneros explores the tide of unhappy feelings that wash over a child when, on her eleventh birthday, a teacher ("Mrs. Price") forces her to accept ownership of someone else's hideous sweater. It had been hanging, unclaimed, in the coat closet for months. At first, the girl is intimidated, speechless. Then in a small voice she attempts to tell Mrs. Price that the ratty sweater isn't hers. To her dismay, the teacher dismisses her truth,

> "Of course it's yours," Mrs. Price says, "I remember you wearing it once." Because she's older and the teacher, she's right and I am not.

The child loathes the sweater. It's old. It smells. It revolts her. *She does not want it.* Her protest happens emotionally, in a way that many of us will appreciate:

> Not mine, not mine, not mine, but Mrs. Price is already turning to page thirty-two, and math problem number one. I don't know why but all of a sudden I'm feeling sick inside like the part that's three wants to come out of my eyes, only I squeeze them shut tight and bite down on my teeth real hard and try to remember that today I'm eleven, eleven....
>
> But when the sick feeling goes away and I open my eyes, the red sweater's still sitting there, like a big red mountain. I move the red sweater to the corner of my desk with my ruler. I move my pencil and books and eraser as far from it as possible. I even move my chair a little to the right. Not mine, not mine, not mine.[5]

The "I Am" within the girl refuses so much as to touch what is false. She recoils from a lie. She gets sick. She cries. These expressions are all variants of positive protest. When dissent flows from a wish to be heard or gain a semblance of security it is designed to structure the integrity of wholesome autonomy.

Positive rebellion is not necessarily defiance, as an anecdote shared by presidential historian Doris Kearns-Goodwin reveals. Apparently, John F. Kennedy Jr.'s mother was instrumental in encouraging her son's authenticity. Although JFK Jr. was clearly the child of both his mother and father, Goodwin writes

> Jackie was so determined from the time he was little to make him his own person and to have him walk a separate path from the Kennedy tradition.... The story that keeps coming back to me is that story of the time he was a little kid and he's crying on the slopes when he's skiing [because he's fallen down] and Bobby [Kennedy] comes over to him and says, "Kennedys don't cry." ... And [John-John] said, "*This* Kennedy cries."[6]

It takes great fortitude for a young child to contradict an esteemed uncle about a value the whole family wants him to learn — particularly if that uncle is charismatic and viewed as a father figure. Nevertheless, to swallow one's true feelings (and hold back tears) amounts to a sneak attack on the self. A few such assaults on a child's integrity can produce the reflex that educator Herbert Kohl calls "willed not-learning": the lack of assent in learning. For Kohl, as it would seem for Robert Lindner and

Alice Miller, not-learning can signify healthy protest. Kohl explains:

> Over the years I've known many youngsters who chose to actively not-learn what their school, society, or family tried to teach them. Not all of them were potential victims of their own choices to not-learn. For some not-learning was a strategy that made it possible for them to function on the margins of society instead of falling into madness or total despair. It helped them build a small, safe world in which their feelings of being rejected by family and society could be softened. Not-learning played a positive role and enabled them to take control of their lives and get through difficult times.[7]

Another well-documented example of unruly but positive protest involves Helen Keller. Before the age of six, preoccupied as she was with sheer physical survival, Helen Keller thought with her body. Later she described herself as having lacked "one spark of emotional or rational thought."[8] Keller's primitive behavior could have been viewed as revolt. She used tears and anger; she raged, kicked, and grabbed at things like food to obtain creature comforts. Were those outbursts rebellion or simply Keller's finest, and only, means of survival and healthy growth?

Abused children who flee to family shelters generally achieve better results from that "rebellion" than those who crudely strike out at their offender. Not always. If neat and tidy rules for rebellion existed, surely someone would have published a manual by now. Running away can be a life-affirming—maybe life-saving—strategy. As a performing artist admitted in an interview, "The further away from home I went, the more confident I became."

Some adults fail to distinguish between the positive and negative variables of protest. Others want only what's conventionally best for the child and unwittingly snuff out authentic drives. Mature, democratically inclined adults discern the *feelings* beneath children's protests and learn to interpret their nonverbal signals like

- sullen looks or silence,

- disdainful shrugs,

- moodiness,

- refusal to joke or join in family humor,

- crying,

- withdrawal,

- rebuffing shows of affection,

- sarcasm,

- rudeness.

By example, not harangue, do adults teach children to express appropriately the needs at the seat of their soul. They also give a child

- wide latitude in sensitive areas of expression, such as the area of obvious talent,

- help in releasing anger constructively,

- guidance in the communicative arts and risk taking,

- information about what factors make one action or tone of voice fruitful and another counterproductive.

## Adults as Servant-Mentors

It is an adult's responsibility to serve the needs of children. Too many adults still view girls and boys as objects, as their possessions or investments that somehow are supposed to result in a tangible return on effort expended. The old saying that children should support us and be a comfort to us in our old age sums up the last idea. Some parents forget that parenthood is not a lifetime job. Long after an appropriate chronological age, they smother or overwhelm their adult children, who variously cooperate in the deleterious dance. Ironically, it's a rare offspring that doesn't crave ongoing friendship with a parent or elder-mentor, if the bonds of affection run deep and true. Spiritual mentors help boys and girls enliven society through their inborn gifts.

French novelist Father Jean Sulivan helpfully reminds us that most major religions initially were founded on something other than "family values." Jesus of Nazareth, Lao-Tsu, Buddha and Confucius were not focused on parental comforts or child-rearing but on Ultimate Reality. The archetypical spiritual leader tends to make an early existential choice to leave the family fold, to seek rebirth in union with absolute Transcendence.

Sulivan asks us to bless the happy childhood that lets a girl or boy grow up independently while feeling unconditionally loved:

> Let family life be intense but brief, aimed at healthy pain and new birth. For everything tends to substitute itself for the material womb in order to keep us in the cave of illusion: money, art, pleasure (when it leaves no place for joy), love (if it's only a remedy for

boredom), religion (when it mollycoddles us), every memory, happy or unhappy, that walls us up within individuality. We are not yet born.[9]

## *Productive Aggression vs. Undue Compliance*

The spark to forge ahead, to transcend the "material womb," is essential to sheer survival. Self-trust is an ingredient of all of that. Paradoxically we often develop that confidence in the throes of messy situations. We know that "perfection" in family life is nonexistent. Moreover, a large number of creative children tend to emerge from marginally disrupted homes.

Idiosyncratic, inconsistent parents can nevertheless raise inspired youngsters. Parents who see-saw between rigidity and flexibility, or who are so frazzled in their own right that they ignore a child, at least don't concentrate exclusively on their young. Frequently, in untidy set-ups children gain a relaxed view of the chinks in their own armor. They embrace their off-beat goals. They accept others' flaws. Left to themselves, they'll tap into their inventive energy at a young age. Or learn to think through problems on their own. Or perhaps become easy-going enough to take uncommon risks: write a letter to a parent explaining a problem (instead of avoiding or directly doing battle with the parent); rebel against some teacher's unfairness; confront a bully; quit a dull school course; reject a manipulative pal. As we saw, even failing at something deemed significant by adults can be a form of productive rebellion.

Children may possess a high IQ without having an impulse for spontaneous, positive protest. They seek safety in convention. They're outer-directed. They prize obedience and structure above the joyful chaos of authentic growth. This is antilife.

Typically, parents of such youngsters are conforming too. They value and try to program the compliant worldview. The entire family cherishes life in what Sulivan termed the "cave of illusion" — with short-term, obvious rewards — above vital engagement with vital goals. Offspring are taught to

- keep up with appearances,
- make a good impression on others,
- value outer success above the integrity of the core self.

Sons and daughters who are mentored into the art of superficials generally strive for good grades or a high-paying career at the expense of inner dynamism. That's how the overly compliant become self-punishing. To substitute the term "self-sheltering" for the word "rebellion" might help us fathom the inspired depths of certain youthful protests.

A well-publicized experiment in subjugation underscores how undue compliance grants ruinous power to those in authority. A psychology professor set up a mock prison in the basement of the psych department. He recruited twenty-four students, arbitrarily dividing them into "guards" and "prisoners." The professor noted that each group quickly assumed the mind-set of the role being played: Volunteer guards tended to be intimidating. Some grew inhuman. Volunteer prisoners tended to relinquish their most basic civil rights. Anyone could have quit participating at any time or walked out of their "cells" to rejoin friends and families. Instead, many gave up their identities, freedom of movement, ability to do such elementary things as bathe regularly, buy soft drinks from a vending machine, or smoke whenever they chose. Some accepted solitary confinement (e.g., in closets) for minor infractions of rules. In effect, fright and learned helplessness (i.e., a true victim's mien) developed in a snap.

A tough volunteer-guard recalls:

> There was a time when I said, "How far will these prisoners let me go?" Because the one thing I noticed about them is that they never stood up for themselves and their own rights or dignities. And all any prisoner would have to say is, "Hey, this is an experiment, knock it off, OK?" And I would have stopped.

When one student prisoner was asked why he and the others didn't simply give up the ordeal, he answered, "We just forgot to say, 'I quit'... No one ever said, 'I quit.'"

The professor who initiated the project assumed the role of prison superintendent and admitted that he, too, succumbed to the cruelty of the environment.[10] The more restrictive the atmosphere in the mock prison became, the less able were volunteers to contemplate taking independent steps to leave. This example reinforces Bettelheim's notion: Fear cripples wholesome autonomy.

### Learning from Early Awakeners: The Principle of Self-Sheltering

To spiritually intelligent children (and to the adults they become) if external success, no matter how dazzling, denies the integrity of the core self it is tantamount to suicide. As we have seen in school shootings across the United States, when youngsters murder others it's likely that, first, they'll have snuffed out their own vital life: the animating principle or élan vital within. Deadness cannot abide what's living. I believe that to understand youngsters who at a tender age kill parents, their classmates, or themselves, we must search for the "extreme situation" in their lives.

The overly compliant, depressed, or enraged child casts light on adult self-sabotage and despair. The self-punitive reflex seems to have caused even a spiritual giant like Tolstoy to consider suicide. Although he never believed what his elders' taught him about the importance of fame and wealth, Tolstoy labored to embody those values in adulthood. He achieved worldly success, adopting a half-hearted religion in the process. He forged a seemingly happy marriage, had beautiful children, and achieved material security at the expense of his original, uncomplicated boyhood wish to be virtuous. Having consciously chosen against himself, in his fifties his life felt meaningless:

> It [came] to this, that I, a healthy, fortunate man, felt I could no longer live: some irresistible power impelled me to rid myself one way or another of life. I cannot say I *wished* to kill myself. The power which drew me away from life was stronger, fuller and more widespread than any mere wish. It was a force similar to the former striving to live, only in a contrary direction.... And all this befell me at a time when all around me I had what is considered complete good fortune.[11]

Tolstoy returned to his simple, boyhood intent. After experiencing a serious depression, he protested — corrected his way, beginning a search for God and life-meaning. At last he remembered, "I only lived at those times when I believed in God."[12] We learn from Tolstoy that

- healthy protest is always an option (Tolstoy activated his healthiest choices in midlife);

- our so-called "wrong" choices — our delays, missteps, embarrassing blunders or failures — could be unconscious ploys of self-sheltering;

- our vision of some holy, whole, ideal is often quite ordinary, unspectacular, and traceable to childhood's dreams of the good life.

It helps to recall our conduct the first time we felt overwhelmed by an outside threat. Were we so intimidated that speech eluded us? Did we hide, run, throw a fit, get sick, cry, lock ourselves in a room, or try too hard to please? What youthful strategies did we employ when feeling vulnerable, or attempting to meet our needs or protect ourselves? To locate a higher meaning in our shards of childhood protest, we locate the patterns of intuitive strategies by which we shielded ourselves when we lacked adult means. Even our mature choices, masks, or pet responses are best understood as a symmetry of the interior life, a delicate language unto itself. Like the tongue of dreams or poetry, the parlance of self-shielding can be learned.

Many of us, as adults, sense our shine was dulled long ago. But we feel a glow of genuineness radiating beneath our guilt, fear, or anger. By observing our productive mentors, even from afar, we can glean significant cues about our authenticity. Most frequently no spoon-feeding or personal meetings are required. We are gathering threads of information about attributes that we desire, weaving a patchwork quilt of valued qualities. Broadcaster David Essel examines that sort of transaction in his poem "Silent Teacher." The narrator's "heart is touched by the creases on the face" of an old guitar player. Although musician and admirer sit at a distance from one another, a lasting, silent learning transpires:

> No words spoken
> Volumes said.[13]

To assess our ability to guide and mentor our own or our children's spiritual gifts and to enhance productive "rebellion" we can ask whether we and they

- recognize and express what's needed,
- intuitively reject whatever or whoever tries to harm them,
- watch for the verbal or nonverbal "No,"
- learn the "secret" often illogical language of inspired self-sheltering.

Long past childhood, as I approached my thirties, I was still auditing myself in all these areas of positive rebellion. What had superficially *seemed* traitorous was, over the long haul of life, a spiritual necessity. I came to agree with Erich Fromm that learning to love life requires our actively avoiding what's phoney and staying clear of the orbit of "zombies...whose soul is dead."[14] Furthermore, as author Carolyn Heilbrun proposes in *Writing a*

*Woman's Life,* women express their power and leadership as they tell the truth about, and with, their lives.

So great a saint as Augustine admitted that long past boyhood he was "carried away to vanities...when men were set before him as models" glorying in their own disordered lives.[15] We who awaken to our intuitive wisdoms in adulthood must have heart. Rarely are we too ancient to yield to the idiosyncratic conduct that leads to spiritual integrity. It takes wisdom to follow the psalmist's advice, to avoid the way of pretenders, and to dwell instead under the pinions and shelter of the Almighty.

That we parents, teachers, or others feel inconvenienced by boys and girls' self-sheltering behavior is irrelevant, unless we block their holy shine. Then, shame on us.

# Chapter Ten

# Early Reconcilers

*Mostly I think I'm shy.*
— Student, age sixteen

In 1998, when the United Methodist Church in Barrington, Illinois, burned down, the pastor was approached by a little girl he'd never seen before. As he surveyed the charred ruins Chelsea Sigmond, age seven of North Barrington, dished out a five-dollar donation (her allowance money) saying, "I just wanted to help you fix the church." Chelsea had planned to use her savings to buy a key chain, but after watching the story about the fire on TV she changed her mind: "I just felt sad and wanted to give some of my allowance.... After that I felt really warm and happy inside."[1]

Is it only the rare youngster who defers gratification? Do only unusual children assume unnecessary obligations or forgive? Perhaps we simply ignore the countless expressions of spiritual intelligence all around us in every age and socioeconomic group.

By definition, early awakeners are *aware:* Their viewpoint is widened by the inner press to move beyond a programmed narrowness. They are our "cheerful givers." They sense interrelatedness. They offer the new kid on the block a chance to join an established circle of friends. They are our shocking sharers who loan their new shiny bikes to neighbors or give away trinkets we feel are too valuable to forgo. Whenever a young person notices a need or an injustice and addresses it courageously, sweetly, it's the result of some press of the Spirit within.

Inspired youngsters pay attention to their tugs of conscience. They hand over to someone needy the coins they've been saving for a special treat. Or respond intuitively to a perceived threat. We have seen that they *choose* to help themselves achieve meaningful goals, thereby serving us from their interior wealth. One child serves by relinquishing a coveted key chain in favor of some larger communal good. Another serves by undertaking a seemingly thankless task to teach the world around him what it means to have AIDS.

These wide-ranging purposes appear to have little in common. In fact, all choices are unified at the level of consciousness that drives them. The higher the awareness, the more spiritual the direction. As we intentionally nullify negative emotions — fear, covetousness, self-centeredness — we spot options with the eyes of our heart. That means any young person can reconcile a conflict of any size by stripping away normal conceits, the interior betrayals that hint, "I can't do this. I'm lacking in power," or the feelings of contempt that suggest, "No one but me is worthy or can be trusted." In the angst of their conscious tugs-of-war, little children address the tensions between their safety needs and their growth choices. The spiritually intelligent inch toward the sacred drives of their own humanity.

## *Overview: Early Reconciliations*

At the crest of early conflicts children arrive at a cross-road. They look at a matter and notice several ways to turn. Here's when they wonder, "Which way is best?" "Can I express what I sense I value? Can I trust myself?" "Do I dare do thus and such?" "What will happen if . . . ?" Chelsea Sigmond surprised everyone when she donated her allowance to Pastor Wilson. She had been riding in the car with her mother when they passed by the church, and she asked if they could stop. Her request seems to have been fueled by a spontaneous spark of generosity.

Feeling compassionate, articulating what was wanted to her mother, a significant authority figure, on an important issue gave Chelsea a chance to reconcile contradictions: to give up one thing valued for something else of higher worth. An infinite range of decision-points confronts each youngster. One gives away coins; another teases from her mind the germ of an idea for a poem she wants to write; a third flees some household brutality. A writer with an abusive parent told me he simply decided to "take care of business first" and deal with any negative consequences later:

> Dying emotionally wasn't in my plans. Sure I left. That's a given for someone like me. I told myself I'd deal with the guilt later. Guilty conscience or not, survival required that I move in with relatives who, thankfully, understood and took me in.

Only self-betrayal denies the obvious: for instance, that things are absurd at home or dangerous or that a teacher is bullying us at school or that, more than anything else, we love God or that we'll use our life to express some representation of beauty. Confronted by such realities, if we convince ourselves no conscious choice is needed, we stop growing spiritually.

Since awakening is the true business of life, whoever dies to the false or illusory existence is more alive than before, fired up, reconstituted and hungry for yet more life. The earlier example of children called "little old souls" also reveals much about the attribute of reconciliation.

## Peaceful Movings-On

"Shake the dust off your feet," advised Jesus of Nazareth to his disciples when counseling them how to respond to unfriendly receptions. Little old souls intuitively receive — and follow — that same superordinate directive. In most cases, no one actively teaches children "how" to remedy their tensions or choose a peaceable, yet self-protective response to trouble.

To "reconcile" means, in part, to overlook, to settle, to restore to union. Forgiveness, then, is a critical ingredient of all reconciliation. To forgive is to give up a claim against. One acknowledges the thing to be overlooked. There's ample evidence that children do overlook torment. They cannot but love their parents, siblings, and important others. Their greater challenge, perhaps like ours, may be to handle the anger they feel, to get over it. That's like crossing a bridge in a storm. To get to the other side, you must walk *over* the troubled waters. After that, shaking the dust off the feet becomes your new norm, your unattachment to the old trouble, old feelings, the old narrowness that would provoke or expect the other to comply. Forgiveness is a shift to new norms. It lets us move on.

## Personal Patterns

Here's what made me move on. Sandwiched between my parents' civility and their bedrock of mutual respect was a deepening substratum of turmoil. Neither I nor anyone could help my mother — not family, not physicians, assuredly not the squad of psychiatrists who seemed to get caught up in her confusion. My father was busy — remote, ever absent, ever traveling, and now in dire financial straits. He was suffering, too. My brother, now living full-time at a military school, must have felt much lonelier.

Had there been someone to turn to, how helpful would conversation have been? The well-bred did not discuss their private concerns. At least in our nest one managed friction by looking away. To me, that was the real insanity. One knows what one knows. But I could not — would not — tell you with a straight face that I was thinking about forgiveness. More pressing survival thoughts held my attention. Furthermore, I'm certain forgiveness has not been my greatest challenge. However much I sought to avoid my mother, I never felt she meant me any intentional harm. I was grappling with other oppressive emotions, such as overblown feelings of responsibility to take care of things, including myself.

Frankly, I sensed myself carrying precious cargo and deserving of stable conditions. Deeper still, the constant disarray blocked lovelier, more intelligent realities that beckoned. Directly upon hearing the news of my father's heart attack, I ran away to my best friend's house (I'll call her "S."), whose home had become a temporary emotional haven.

S.'s family was dysfunctional, too, but all such terms are relative. At least her crew listened to each other and had ritualized some homey, predictable routines. S.'s mother was a wide-bodied ex-actress, probably a practicing alcoholic, with bleached straw-yellow hair, a thick Southern drawl, and, whenever she emerged from her bedroom, an incredibly nurturing grain. That family thoroughly enjoyed their food. They ate round-the-clock, feeding all strays and wayfarers who happened by, cooking hamburgers on their grill, nonstop. Ground round, seared, was their fare of choice for every conceivable meal and snack, and their house stayed ever-pungent with the scent of charbroiled meat.

The day my father died, S. and I and her cozy, boozy mother, perpetually clad in a hot-pink terry robe, sat around their white Formica table. We scarfed up burgers and wept openly about my loss. Memorable smatterings of comfort. They'd have let me stay, but not forever. A jumble of rage and grief drove me to their home. Common sense dragged me back to my house a few measly hours later. I had nowhere else to go. Right then it hit me that my goal wasn't just to dream about a more lasting escape. It was to achieve a decent life. To make the effort.

One month later, my demand to live at yet another odious boarding school paid off. As these things go, the new place was pretty nice: a rambling hacienda affair in sunny California, replete with lush grounds, palomino horses and two aging boxer dogs with tumors on their mouths the size of Nebraska. It was also culturally progressive.

The founder and on-site headmaster, an ex-vaudevillian Danny Kaye look-alike, had a flair for the performing arts and an irreverent sense of humor. High school found me tap dancing, studying philosophy, and taking advanced placement classes on film at U.S.C. I had lucked out again.

Admittedly even before my father died, I'd decided to leave home. His demise was simply my last straw. Without a responsible adult in the house, it was time to go. I repeat that this plotting to escape was not, as you might imagine, a confused mish-mash of wishful, childish thinking. It was intense resolve to protect life's promise. And that intent only strengthened as home events unfolded. However involuntary my mother's problems were, I was unwilling to get sucked into her alien reality. After the age of thirteen, except for one unfortunate summer, I never again lived with my mother.

I did live with a mix of feelings — relief mostly, and inexpressible sadness, and a floating anxiety that came and went without warning, and also heady excitement — all streaming together like a watercolor rainbow painted on wet paper where the red, blue, and yellow bleed into each other. Reconciliation came years later, only after I caught my breath and, through marriage, dropped anchor in years of stability with an intact and loving family, then had therapy, and later still had forged a contemplative life of my own. Forgiveness meant sorting out and overlooking and reinterpreting anew. It intensified with each fresh realization of just how much I have been forgiven and loved.

Here I part company with the moral-imperative crowd. What shell-shocked soldier, freshly home from Vietnam, is freed from distress simply by being admonished: "Snap out of it. You have a duty to family and society. Forget what you've seen and just get on with it now that you're safe and sound." Memory of severe trauma has its subjective side, its perceptual networks of anticipated dangers that can become reflexive. One subtle reminder of long past horrors, and sensitive souls are back in the original trenches.

I believe that, over time, contemplative disciplines, practiced faithfully, wash clean those diskettes of mind. Praying in the Spirit, reflecting on Scripture, spending time in nature, playing with a beloved child, caring for a garden, chickens, a frog pond — these deliver the peace that passes understanding. Of course, that peace is accompanied by divine forgiveness. How could it not be?

## Trials Aid Reconciliation

Having first disclosed tidbits of my personal history in 1990, I wasn't surprised to receive letters from high-achieving readers describing similarly disordered childhoods.[2] They learned to accept their and others' flaws without rancor or inordinate compulsion to follow suit. True, they carried scars. But scars are generally forgotten (until pointed out). Once having vowed to create a better life, they invested their energies productively. No one spent precious time retaliating.

We all agreed: Early heartache motivated us to build a solid family life or a decent career, a point of view, and inner and outer sufficiency. Our necessary capital for those ventures came from the rubble of early hurts, not in a Pollyannaish way, but as a mining process that extracted Helen Keller's nugget: "The hilltop hour would not be half so wonderful if there were no dark valley to traverse." Sometimes traversing dark valleys means striving. Sometimes it requires waiting. Always, though, the good life demands trust and forgiveness. These two attributes, while probably seeded in childhood, require maturity to produce lasting fruit.

The adults who wrote to me identified with the profile of that small band of youngsters acknowledged earlier, the resilient ones that psychologists now call alternatively "invulnerables" and "invincibles." These children thrive despite (maybe because of) their depressing early circumstances, exhibiting numerous adaptive skills such as

- insightful reading of people and their environment,

- spotting opportunities and deftly improvising their way to them,

- becoming adequate adults because they must, because as children their own well-being depended on wit, self-counsel, and the knack of locating trustworthy adults for assistance.[3]

I'd guess those like a James Baldwin or a Christy Brown accept an adult's mentoring only after they've intuited that this or that other is *worth* listening to. Spiritual intelligence lights the way. Whoever trusts the light walks in its glow and learns by doing.

Countless numbers share my experience of breaking free of childhood turmoil, and no one rejects a family without good reason. Youngsters usually will abandon only a parent who, long before, has abandoned them. Thus they correct what's already gone awry. Early awakeners take reparative action before the situation harms them any further. Fear, anger, or guilt may become life-time companions, but I sense that the more intense the inner shine, the greater degree of forgiving abandon an individual demonstrates. In this regard, I heard a lecturer once admit he'd been liberated in peace the minute he visited his parent's grave — a parent who had abandoned him — and said, "From this day forth, I'll send only love to you." Even a child eventually can realize you can't force a parent (or anyone else) to change, and that outlook furthers harmony.

## Being the Spiritual Parent We Seek

Harvard psychologist Samuel Osherson, writing about men and their fathers, suggests that it is possible for a man to (a) examine the anger and disappointment felt toward a father even when the parent is absent, (b) heal himself without reconciliation with the father, and (c) establish a surface friendship with the father, but without healing himself. I'd propose that all of the above is a genderless, universal truth, applicable to anyone. Spiritual intelligence undergirds all true healing. It alone eradicates separateness and prompts understanding of our shared human condition. Moreover, forgiveness has less to do with rubbing elbows with our offenders than it does with cultivating a deep empathy for everyone's underlying humanity — ours included. Inspired thought and distance from the abuse reveals that our *own* healing is inextricably tied to our forgiveness of others. Only a brute or an ignoramus forces a child — like Kimitake, let's say — to live with and nurse a deranged or corrupting elder. Physical distance from damage is critical to a child's protection or anyone's sanctified purposes. Who, for example, asks a beaten wife to continue living with her murderous spouse? Why then do we not better protect children? Distance offers necessary shelter from any reign of terror. Even with spaces of time and safety there can be lots to "overlook." Borrowing Osherson's terminologies, reconciliation comes as we are able to

(a) understand the always poignant reasons why the past was the way it was (thus liberating ourselves from a self- and worldview fixated on betrayal by another), and

(b) heal — make whole — the wounded parent in our hearts (thus growing into a reflection of wholeness ourselves, a richer, fuller expression of the right, or spiritual, idea ever-present within ourselves).[4]

There are as many variations to these two accomplishments as there are individuals. I'd also add a third, healing, reconciling solution that seems to integrate the two items above. We can

(c) *be* the spiritually illumined parent, the good shepherd, we so longed for when we were young.

Here are several sketches that expand the last point.

### Traits of the Good Spiritual Parent

In the foreword to John Muir's autobiography, David Quammen writes that Muir's is a story of "one young man's climb out of hell." There were, Quammen relates, two hellish pits:

One was metaphorical: the dispiriting drudgery of
seventeen-hour days at hard labor on a frontier farm,
with no time for schooling or reading or enjoy-
ment of the wild landscape, and no reason to expect
that, however hard a man worked....And one [pit]
was literal: a ninety-foot well shaft, chiseled down
through fine-grain sandstone. The young Muir was
consigned to both those pits by his father, a Bible-
thumping authoritarian who threatened to be the
nemesis of John's life.[5]

Yet as we read of John's boyhood we find no bitterness in
him. He is objective, kindly even, and "guided by fairness
and restraint, if not forgiveness [and] animated by the
joy of small blessings — especially those blessings derived
from contact with nature."[6]

At his father's deathbed, there sat John — holding old
Daniel Muir's hand. More than that, John Muir's life and
his contributions shepherded others into an understanding of authentic peace. That's good spiritual parenting: to
serve humanity by becoming the nurturing, respectful parent one longs for. That's my point: A life's vocation heals
so much. It completes a circle, drawing us to supernatural
Love, for "His hands maketh whole." Good spiritual
parents fulfill their own purposes while, simultaneously,
paving the way — *through* those purposes — for others to
complete theirs.

I once overheard a movie director say that he entered
his profession to prove to himself that good fathering was
possible. Apparently he'd grown up with an absentee father and today realizes a wholeness of stewardship by
being as fully present and steadfast as possible with his

young actors. That's also good spiritual parenting. We serve others with our legacy but also by the run of our daily affairs. There's a conscious, constructive synergy at play in good stewardship.

A reader wrote to me saying her parents had tried to kill her. She believes she came to grips with their twisted behavior only *after* realizing she loved them. Then she forgave them. She did not, however, forget an ongoing danger. They still lash out, still pretend what happened didn't, still deny responsibility. With great presence of mind she refuses to have a hypocritical relationship with them and continually revisits her intent to forgive. As if preparing us for that lifelong exercise in choosing the way of harmony, the Bible instructs us to forgive endlessly.

The good spiritual parent I sense we wanted (and most want to be) maturely demonstrates many attractive traits, for instance,

- affirming life in self and others,
- choosing the path of peace,
- using creative endeavors to bring some greater good into being, thereby empowering others,
- seeing the heartache or a nemesis as a teacher of sorts,
- relinquishing false guilts and helping others do likewise.

## False Guilt Relinquished as an Aid to Forgiveness

Between my mother and me, absolution was always a given. To understand this, you may have to be a mother — or have known mine. My mother accepted my failings with a love that was incapable of holding these against me. Whatever transpired over the years, we felt deep affinity for one another. If you've ever marveled at the way buds sprout for the bloom after a long harsh winter, that's how it now seems. Eventually, we found ways to utter the inexpressible: unconditional love had lived with us all through the years. No dramatic showdown was involved. Seemingly out of the blue, when she was in her eighties, my mother and I had one of those effortless exchanges where all was released. Whatever tumultuous emotions swam on the surface of memory, underneath were the everlasting arms of divine love. Things settled down. Love completed our circle. Or, at least, my heart is satisfied. As that's a linchpin to the peace we crave, I'll return to the subject momentarily.

Looking back I see that all our lives we were teaching each other about forgiveness.

I think that all along the two of us understood the profundity of Thomas Merton's healing framework: In the scheme of eternity our reconciliations have always existed. Like love, forgiveness simply *is* — from before the beginning. Our human ruptures do not matter, for "in the joy of being known and forgiven, we find it so much easier to forgive everything, even before it happens."[7]

We forgive each other when we sense we have been forgiven — or given — much. Our reconciliations are more likely when

(a) our early environment promotes simple human respect and

(b) we lay hold of the obvious: We mortals are inconsistent.

Mine was a gentle family with a good and decent nature. That doesn't mean I wouldn't find ways to protect myself all over again, if need arose. It means that I learned about forgiveness, in part, by being influenced by two generous adults who valued kindness. I loved the fact that my parents never spoke a prejudicial word against each other or against me or any race or ethnic group — even in the worst of times. What's more, I never encountered a shred of vulgarity, meanness, or bigotry before coming to America. This is an astonishing statement considering that I grew up in the midst of bombs dropping and a world war rooted in vicious racism. The hate was simply outside of our home, and we all knew it.

The first antiethnic slur I ever heard was on my first day in the U.S., at age six, riding in a taxi on the streets of San Francisco. Our driver shouted a racist curse at an old, bowed-over Asian man hobbling through the intersection too slowly for the cabby's liking.

Another illustration: My father, an expansive, freedom-loving man, suffered in concentration camp. For all I know he'd been brutalized. On his release, he was driven directly to a hospital and remained there for months. Just as my mother refused to discuss her convent years, so my father kept silent about his time as a prisoner of war. Somehow he came to terms with the "extreme situation" and after the war quickly resumed harmonious business ties with all his Asian associates, the Japanese included. When it comes to human inconsistencies, well, we have only to examine ourselves. We can and do love those who hurt us. We can and do hurt those who love us. We can and do forgive everything — even before it happens.

## Accepting Inconsistencies

It has become fashionable (if also irksome) to hear grown
people rant against their parents for having had the au-
dacity to be flawed. We hear little about, or from, those
who remain relatively patient and who were relatively
conscious as children. Early awakeners reconcile themselves to the fact that both they and their parents are
human: flawed, lovely beings embodying a lavish complex of ironies. These children accept contradictions, for
instance, that the same parents who genuinely adore
them at one moment (when swept away by affection)
may, at the very next moment, genuinely fear, hate, or
ignore them. While they accept those opposing qualities, that could also necessitate shaking the dust off
their feet.

Forgiveness does not automatically spell intimate "fel-
lowship." I stress this given a silly societal expectation
that to forgive destines us to stroll down Bonding Lane,
arm in arm with those who continually harm us. I
think not.

The spiritual patterns I've described suggest that some
children can embrace the vagaries and contradictions of
their own and others' clumsy, often endearing, humanity.
Others require years of maturing before they can hold in
mind two or more opposing ideas: that they and others
possess conflicting qualities, and that they must own that
paradox, live comfortably with it, and that reconciliation
means integration — not splitting off the "good" from
the "bad."[8] As spiritual intelligence increases so does our
comfort with life-as-it-is.

## Accepting Life's Purpose

My robustly creative friends tell me they fought against the notion, as did I, that youth's function is to satisfy parental wants. Each one who flourished somehow found strength enough to honor the divinity within, the inner voice that commands, "Honor Me. Be faithful to who I Am." Those I've observed losing their way lost it long ago, either by idealizing some authority figure (thereby relinquishing too much power), or by laminating onto their pain an unreflective cheeriness, or by affirming the *concept* of duty or love more than they concretely affirmed life. Resilient, inspired individuals sustain optimism in the face of obvious unfairness, disappointment, and a family's impaired, jagged relationships. Almost everyone I know manages all that swimmingly, with quiet, uneventful dignity and courage.

A teacher-entrepreneur discovered, in her primary-school years no less, that she and her parents lacked a common ground for true rapport. She could never have a dialogue from the heart with them. For her part, she required solitude and wanted a self-expressive, somewhat intellectual life. She accepted her life's purpose, determining not to blindly follow her parents' path:

> My mother was married at seventeen. Her schooling ended by the eighth grade; my father didn't finish, either. He's a factory worker, as was his father before him. Mom and Dad settled down in the same town in which my dad was born. He doesn't really speak to the family with words — lives on the edge of things, sits on the sidelines — especially now that he's losing his hearing. Our lack of communication is painful, in

a way. When talk veers toward deeper issues, beyond the details of everyday life, I feel I lose my mother, who looks at me as though she doesn't get it. It could be a matter of vocabulary, but I don't think so. My parents' world is what it's always been, and they've had trouble accepting new ideas.

Our relationship today is what it's always been. By age five or six I had a sense that said, "I'm probably different from the others, not meant to live like they do." That idea has always been with me as a subtle knowing. It's always been in me.

That's the type of ongoing trial that fires up the creative purposes of early awakeners, intensifies the will to survive, flourish, or achieve some mighty dream of destiny.

## A Blessed Chaos

As we saw in the lives of Helen Keller, Hermann Hesse, and John Muir, grief or frustration can fuel that dream. In other cases, enduring calm or familial affection paves the way.

At any rate, my own youth was decidedly a mixed bag. It overflowed with love and turbulence, with soaring moods and low, with privilege and deprivation, with buoyant, glittery times and gloom. We had it all. I took each excruciating turn to heart, and then used it to decode my world and, to be sure, myself. Such efforts put me in fabulous company.

Spiritually bright, creative achievers commonly endure a conflicted youth. Occasionally the family nest is idyllic. More often these homes are not models for the Brady Bunch. In the Goertzels' studies of the eminent, the parents of famous people were typically traumatized or deprived. Their lives were full of emotional turmoil, including the "extreme situation." The high-achieving progeny of pained or eccentric adults had free rein over their own interests, in part, because their elders were usually preoccupied with private upheavals or fascinations. Moreover, these children were described as "comfortably disorderly, sloppy, anarchic, chaotic, vague, doubtful, uncertain, indefinite, approximate, inexact, or inaccurate" and as having less need than most to be pleasing and commonly indifferent as to what the world thought of them.[9] Wholesome development involves a lot of choosing-and-arranging.

## Learning about Love's Forgiveness

In the aftermath of a preschool shooting in California, members of the Los Angeles police force were televised shepherding toddlers out of harm's way. The gunman had fled the scene. The officers didn't know where he was. Incongruously, blue uniformed police, assault weapons drawn, baby-stepped the tots to shelter. Police held children's hands as children held hands with each other. The preschoolers, shaken and mystified, couldn't comprehend why policemen, with guns drawn, had removed them from class. The story circulated that when one of these four-year-olds finally found his mother, he looked up and tremulously asked her, "Did we do something very bad?"

That child's question — his essential innocence — breaks our heart. Most of us feel deeply enough to em-

pathize with the subtlety of his fears because in some
haunting corner of memory we are that child. That debilitating guilt must go. If, like that boy, we heap unnecessary
blame on our shoulders, we'll blame others too for things
that went awry long ago.

What we need is an infusion of spiritual intelligence.
Intimacy with the Spirit is no intellectual exercise, although faith is involved. Prayer, meditation, and other
contemplative disciplines liberate peace because, through
these, we experience peace. Only the Spirit within lifts the
fear and blame that separates us from the compassion we
yearn to feel and to give.

When Julian of Norwich faced her own doubts, "our
good Lord answered" with the assurance that we are
never to despair over our frequent falls. Only if our heart
does not condemn us can we accept such ideas or entertain
a bold confidence toward God (see 1 John 3:21).

Sebastian Moore helpfully proposes that we open up to
the inherent compassion in the divine love if we're willing
to risk our former perceptual system. We've got to unload
the entire old viewpoint to dump our feelings of isolation,
the helplessness born of a wrong mind. The slightest touch
of grace dissolves the old view at its root and draws our
soul into unity and from "that infinite and luminous center" ultimately we find the antidote to separateness and
self-importance. Only the divine forgiveness sets aside the
*entire* false outlook:

> It is not ignoring it, or sweeping it aside, or urging
> me to forget about myself in my Narcissistic wriggle.
> It is getting into the wriggle, liberating the latter's
> captive.... For now there is awakening within me,

as the victim of my meanness, as the bearer of my own life, the spark of true being that belongs in the totality of being.[10]

I am not saying we don't tumble as a matter of course. Most of us are very much like the desert monk in that old story about regression. When asked by visitors how monks spent their time at the monastery, the desert father replied, "We get up and we fall down. We get up and we fall down."

Sacred forgiveness is not really about our frequent falls. It is a gracious, concretely available attribute of divine compassion. With each shower of spiritual insight, a bit more grizzled self-blame washes away, for divine love assures us,

There is no fear in love; but perfect love casts out fear
Because fear involves punishment,
And the one who fears is not perfected in love.

(John 4:18)

In essence, what we can change, we change. What we can't, we live with yet, spiritually, rise above.

# Epilogue

An inspired child is, as we are, human and therefore, humanly speaking, contradictory. Spiritual intelligence does not make children impervious to fear, rage, or feeling separate and different. Memories of mistreatment can take eons to dissolve. The inspired child is at once sure and unsure, powerful and helpless, dependent and autonomous. He or she searches for answers, yet knows something sure, something of unitive truth. No matter how illumined, even saints in childhood do not always devise blemish-free solutions that perfectly neutralize each trauma. As Chekhov reputedly noted, every saint has a past and every sinner a future.

Here it is then, in the young child's awakening, that we find stirrings of spiritual intelligence and future creative health, but no one suggests stainless perfection. Early awakeners are not always aware, not always accepting of their own and others' contradictory impulses, not ever-alert or fully illumined, not even particularly well equipped to fend off the unthinking ineptitudes that can ruin childhood. The qualities of spiritual intelligence — intuitive authority, inspired essence, evolving reconciliations, like wholeness itself — arrive incrementally. Each life seems a work in progress, and some "works" are further along than others.

Here, too, we find the surface yin and the yang of it. Faith and doubt, falling and rising, seeking and knowing are interplays that last until that which is perfect arrives. When the individual utilizes shadow elements in the service of the sacred, nothing is hidden except to be revealed, nor ever been in secret, but that it should come to light (Mark 4:22).

Early awakeners provide patterns of what it means to move into life with virtue. Such girls and boys remind us that our own passage to flawless love, forgiveness, and unity is a holy work and that it is we who are the first fruits, or progression of saintly awakening.

Into this world keeps being born a golden child. Each child is a promise to be redeemed, royalty in the making — despite appearances to the contrary. If we look closely at each one's awakening (yes, even our own) we find the seed of spiritual intelligence and hear our own joy — the laugh we ourselves were born with that lasted as long as we had a perfect faith.[1]

Spiritually speaking, our snapshots of childhood can be symmetrically arranged to make full life's meanings. Then we move on. Rilke once wrote that "for the sake of a single verse" he had had to examine so many things: "the gesture of the flowers," roads in unknown regions, unexpected meetings and "partings one had long seen coming," and a childhood that was still unexplained, including parents whom one had to hurt.[2]

So not for nothing do we sail over youth's landscape. It's life's drill, part of letting go, a slice of transcending. One truthful glance at a memory and the dross disappears so that, lighter, we fly ever higher with the Spirit to heavenly realms. For the sake of our bruised verse, our artistry,

our golden children, we soar over former enchantments,
thirsting for no more than what life really gives: our soul's
primal freedom, that "union of love with love" — that
eternal existence "so delicate and gentle" that there is no
way to describe it.[3]

# Notes

## Introduction

1. R. D. Laing, *The Politics of Experience* (New York: Ballantine Books, 1967), 30.

2. St. Teresa of Avila, *Interior Castle,* trans. E. Allison Peers (Garden City, N.Y.: Doubleday, 1961), 119.

3. Baltasar Gracián y Morales, *The Art of Worldly Wisdom: A Pocket Oracle,* trans. Christopher Maurer (New York: Doubleday, 1992), 168.

## 1. Inspired Thought

1. Daniel Mark Epstein, *Sister Aimee: The Life of Aimee Semple McPherson* (New York: Harcourt Brace Jovanovich, 1993), 15.

2. *Good Morning America,* May 29, 1996 (ABC), *Journal Graphics, Inc.* (transcript), Denver, 11.

3. Albert Camus, *The Rebel: An Essay on Man in Revolt* (New York: Vintage, 1956), 262.

4. Donald Weinstein and Rudolph M. Bell, *Saints and Society* (Chicago: University of Chicago Press, 1982), 29.

5. Richard Bucke, M.D., *Cosmic Consciousness* (New York: E. P. Dutton, 1969), 3–10.

6. Ibid.

7. For a lengthy discussion of unitive consciousness see Marsha Sinetar, *Developing a 21st Century Mind* (New York: Random House, 1991).

8. Marsha Sinetar, *To Build the Life You Want, Create the Work You Love* (New York: Random House, 1997), 171.

9. Meister Eckhart, *The Essential Sermons, Commentaries, Treatises and Defense,* trans. E. Colledge and B. McGinn (New York: Paulist Press, 1961).

10. W. E. Vine, *An Expository Dictionary of New Testament Words* (Nashville: Thomas Nelson, n.d.), 490.

11. John Briggs, *Fire in the Crucible* (Los Angeles: Jeremy P. Tarcher, 1990), 77.

12. Annie Dillard, *An American Childhood* (New York: Harper & Row, 1987), 83.

13. Roald Dahl, *Boy* (London: Penguin Books, 1984), 23.

14. A. Reza Arasteh, *Anxious Search: The Way to Universal Self* (Tehran: Amire Kabir Press, Institute of Perspective Analysis, 1959), 3.

15. For a summary of "time-on-task" literature see Anthony D. Pellegrini and David F. Bjorklund, "The Place of Recess in School:

Issues in the Role of Recess in Children's Education and Development," *Journal of Research in Childhood Education* 11 (Fall–Winter 1996): 5–13.

16. Grace H. Pilon, SBS, *Peace of Mind at an Early Age* (New York: Vantage Press, 1978), 23.

17. Donald Weinstein and Rudolph M. Bell, *Saints and Society* (Chicago: University of Chicago Press, 1982).

18. Richard Bucke, M.D., *Cosmic Consciousness* (New York: E. P. Dutton, 1969), 76.

## 2. Animated Essence

1. Eudora Welty, *One Writer's Beginnings* (New York: Warner Books, 1983), 5.

2. John Briggs, *Fire in the Crucible* (Los Angeles: Jeremy P. Tarcher, 1990), 77.

3. Marsha Sinetar, *A Way without Words* (Mahwah, N.J.: Paulist Press, 1992).

4. For example, Michael J. A. Howe's provocative text, *The Origins of Exceptional Talent* (Cambridge: Blackwell Publishers, 1990), seeks to show that outstanding capabilities are within the reach of nearly everyone, influenced and largely drawn out by environmental factors. It is a highly credible work, well worth a review — particularly for those who prefer a social scientist's view.

5. Briggs, *Fire in the Crucible,* 26.

6. Richard Bucke, M.D., *Cosmic Consciousness* (New York: E. P. Dutton, 1969), 201.

7. Briggs, *Fire in the Crucible,* 9.

8. Silvano Arieti, *Creativity: The Magic Synthesis* (New York: Basic Books, 1976), 346.

9. JoAnn Ridley, *Looking for Eulabee Dix* (Washington, D.C.: National Museum of Women in the Arts, 1997), 24.

## 3. Intuitive Authority

1. I tend to use the word "impersonal" since a divine love is, as Scripture tells us, "irrespective of persons" and also relates to vital mental energy — the sort artists, inventors, even saints tap into when engrossed in, say, creative tasks or praying in the Spirit. However, a friend who worked with psychiatrist Dr. Thomas Hora learned, and liked, the term "nonpersonal" because it implies "the love of being loving."

2. Richard Griswold del Castillo and Richard A. Garcia, *César Chávez: A Triumph of Spirit* (Norman: University of Oklahoma Press, 1995), 11.

3. Silvano Arieti, *Creativity: The Magic Synthesis* (New York: Basic Books, 1976), 26.

4. Henry James and Charles W. Eliot, in *Bartlett's, The Great Quotations* (New York: Lyle Stuart, 1976), 492.

5. Dorothy Ehrhart-Morrison, *No Mountain High Enough: Secrets of Successful African American Women* (Berkeley, Calif.: Conari Press, 1997), 49.

6. Jack Friedman and Bill Shaw, "The Quiet Victories of Ryan White," *People Magazine* (May 30, 1988): 91; and see Cory SerVaas, M.D., "The Happier Days for Ryan White," *Saturday Evening Post* (March 1988): 52–98.

7. Donald Weinstein and Rudolph M. Bell, *Saints and Society* (Chicago: University of Chicago Press, 1982).

8. "Jordan, Barbara C.," *Current Biography Yearbook* (New York: H. W. Wilson, 1993), 289–90.

9. *Current Biography Yearbook*, 289–90.

10. Eugene Herrigel, *Zen in the Art of Archery* (New York: Vintage Books, Random House, 1971), 35.

11. Father William McNamara, "Alive with God" in *For the Love of God: New Writings by Spiritual and Psychological Leaders*, ed. Benjamin Shield and Richard Carlson (San Rafael, Calif.: New World Library, 1990), 109.

12. Vera John-Steiner, *Notebooks of the Mind: Explorations of Thinking* (Albuquerque: University of New Mexico Press, Perennial Library, 1985).

13. Cited in A. Reza Arasteh, *Anxious Search: The Way to Universal Self* (Tehran: Amire Kabir Press, Institute of Perspective Analysis, 1959), 193.

14. Molly Ivins, Del. Eleanor Holmes Norton, "Finally — In Memoriam," *The Newshour,* with Jim Lehrer, January 17, 1996, show no. 5443, transcript by "Strictly Business," Overland Park, Kans., 12–14.

15. Ibid.

16. Ibid.

17. Quote attributed to J. Krishnamurti from unknown source.

18. "Robert Rodriguez," *Rolling Stone* (March 18, 1993): 47.

19. Marsha Sinetar, *Living Happily Ever After* (New York: Villard Books, Random House, 1990).

## 4. Heeding Love

1. David Leeming, *James Baldwin: A Biography* (New York: Alfred A. Knopf, 1994), 6–7.

2. Ibid., 26.

3. Bruno Bettelheim, *Surviving and Other Essays* (New York: Alfred A. Knopf, 1979), 152.

4. It is beyond the scope of this book to detour into a lengthy discussion of this syndrome, the manifestations of which are "as singular as a fingerprint." For an overview of the topic, see Frank M. Ochberg's article on posttraumatic stress therapy in *Psychotherapy* 28, no. 1 (Spring 1999), and also Frank M. Ochberg, ed., *Post-Traumatic Therapy and Victims of Violence* (New York: Brunner/Mazel, 1988), chapter 1.

5. Deirdre V. Lovecky, "Exploring Social and Emotional Aspects of Giftedness in Children," *Roeper Review* 15, no. 1 (September 1992): 18–25.

6. Oliver Sacks, *60 Minutes,* CBS News, New York, vol. 28, no. 18, Burrelle's Transcripts.

7. Wolcott H. Beatty, "The Feelings of Learning," *Childhood Education* 45 (March 1969): 363–69.

8. John Briggs, *Fire in the Crucible* (Los Angeles: Jeremy P. Tarcher, 1990), 80.

9. Ibid.

10. Ibid.

11. Dorothy Day, *The Long Loneliness* (New York: Harper & Row, 1952), 25.

12. Laurie Lisle, *Portrait of an Artist* (New York: Washington Square Press, 1986), 10.

13. See, for example, Rena B. Lewis, Margie K. Kitano, Eleanor W. Lynch, "Psychological Intensities in Gifted Adults," *Roeper Review* (September 1992): 25ff.

14. Lillian Schlissel, *Women's Diaries of the Westward Journey* (New York: Schocken Books, 1992).

15. Joseph Campbell, *Myths to Live By* (New York: Bantam Books, 1972), 47.

16. Claire Gorfinkel, ed., *The Evacuation Diary of Hatsuye Egami* (Pasadena, Calif.: Intentional Productions, 1996), 27–28.

17. Marsha Sinetar, *Ordinary People as Monks and Mystics* (Mahwah, N.J.: Paulist Press, 1986).

18. A. Reza Arasteh, *Anxious Search: The Way to Universal Self* (Tehran: Amire Kabir Press, Institute of Perspective Analysis, 1959), 103.

19. Limiting visitations would seem helpful to children when that supports *their* wishes. A monastic friend adds that there are cases of young people who enter a cloister *because* of parental objections: He says: "This is usually an unconscious decision, and when the parent dies, so does the vocation."

20. Joel Kramer and Diana Alstad, *The Guru Papers* (Berkeley, Calif.: Frog, 1993), 56.

21. Bettelheim, *Surviving and Other Essays,* 253.

22. Ibid., 152.

23. Jane S. Bakerman, "Work Is My Rest," *Conversations with May Sarton,* ed. Carl G. Ingersoll (Jackson: University Press of Mississippi, 1991), 28.

24. Marsha Sinetar, *The Mentor's Spirit* (New York: St. Martin's Press, 1998).

25. William Shakespeare, *Taming of the Shrew,* Act IV, Scene III.

## 5. Rising to the Occasion

1. Laurie Lisle, *Portrait of an Artist* (New York: Washington Square Press, Pocket Books, 1980), 10–11.

2. John Briggs, *Fire in the Crucible* (Los Angeles: Jeremy P. Tarcher, 1990), 41.

3. Lisle, *Portrait of an Artist,* 18–19.

4. Ibid., 18–19.

5. Bruno Bettelheim, *Surviving and Other Essays* (New York: Alfred A. Knopf, 1952), 117.

6. For an educational perspective see Michael Brambring, Friedrich Lösel, and Helmut Skowronek, eds., *Children at Risk: Assessment, Longitudinal Research, and Intervention* (Berlin and New York: Walter de Gruyter, 1989).

7. M. K. Gandhi, *All Men Are Brothers* (New York: Continuum, 1980), 5–7.

8. Erik H. Erikson, *Gandhi's Truth* (New York: W. W. Norton, 1969), 132.

9. Ibid., 119.

10. Ibid., 109.

11. John D. Morse, ed., *Ben Shahn* (New York: Praeger Publishers, 1972), 53.

12. Tom van der Voort and Patti Valkenburg, "Television's Impact on Fantasy Play: A Review of Research," *Developmental Review* 14 (1994): 27–51.

13. Michael D. Davis and Hunter R. Clark, *Thurgood Marshall: Warrior at the Bar, Rebel on the Bench* (New York: Citadel Press Books, 1994), 36–37.

14. Vera John-Steiner, *Notebooks of the Mind: Explorations of Thinking* (Albuquerque: University of New Mexico Press, 1985).

15. Ibid., 220.

16. Ibid.

17. Cited in Briggs, *Fire in the Crucible,* 201.

18. See, for example, Marsha Sinetar, *Living Happily Ever After* (New York: Random House, 1990), and *Developing a 21st Century Mind* (New York: Random House, 1991), where I have charted the constellation of cerebral functions related to whole-seeing.

19. "k. d. lang," *Vanity Fair* 56 (August 1993): 142.

20. E. Paul Torrance, *Guiding Creative Talent* (Englewood Cliffs, N.J.: Prentice-Hall, 1962).

21. *The Press Democrat* (Santa Rosa, Calif.) April 24, 1996, Section A3.

22. Spiritual teachers, and educators, home-schooling parents would do well to study the prototypical school methods in, for example, the Barclay Public School, Montessori Schools, and the Calvert or Waldorf systems.


## 6. Choosing the Best Option

1. Anne Frank, *The Diary of a Young Girl* (New York: Bantam Books, 1993), 171.

2. Rainer Maria Rilke, *Letters to a Young Poet* (New York: W. W. Norton, 1954).

3. Michael D. Davis and Hunter R. Clark, *Thurgood Marshall: Warrior at the Bar, Rebel on the Bench* (New York: Citadel Press Books (Carol Publishing Group), 1994) 38.

4. Ibid., 40.

5. Donald Weinstein and Rudolph M. Bell, *Saints and Society* (Chicago: University of Chicago Press, 1982).

6. Robert Coles, *The Spiritual Life of Children* (New York: Houghton-Mifflin, 1990), 14.

7. Ibid., 10–20.

8. Marsha Sinetar, *The Mentor's Spirit* (New York: St. Martin's Press, 1998).

9. Ibid.

10. Gavin De Becker, *Protecting the Gift* (New York: Dial Press, 1999), 22.

11. Sinetar, *The Mentor's Spirit*.

12. Maya Pines, "Superkids," *Psychology Today* (January 1979).

13. Blanche Wiesen Cook, *Eleanor Roosevelt* (New York: Viking, 1992), 1:11.

14. Bruno Bettelheim, *Surviving and Other Essays* (New York: Alfred P. Knopf, 1979), 116–19.

15. Ibid.

16. Ibid., 116–17.

17. Victor Goertzel and Mildred G. Goertzel, *Cradles of Eminence* (Boston: Little, Brown, 1962).

18. Robert Bolt, *A Man for All Seasons* (New York: Scholastic Books, 1960), 73 (italics in original).

19. Donald Weinstein and Rudolph M. Bell, *Saints and Society* (Chicago: University of Chicago Press, 1982), 59.

20. Jill Ker Conway, ed., *Written By Herself* (New York: Vintage, 1992), 426.

21. E. Paul Torrance, *Guiding Creative Talent* (Englewood Cliffs, N.J.: Prentice-Hall, 1962), 172.

22. Goertzel and Goertzel, *Cradles of Eminence*.

23. Meister Eckhart, *German Works* (New York: Paulist Press, 1981), 258.

## 7. Early Artistry

1. Victor Goertzel and Mildred G. Goertzel, *Cradles of Eminence* (Boston: Little, Brown, 1962).

2. Ibid., 242.

3. Ibid, 243.

4. Jann S. Wenner, "Jagger Remembers," *Rolling Stone* (December 14, 1995): 50.

5. Michael M. Piechowski, "Development of Potential and the Growth of the Self," in *Patterns of Influence on Gifted Learners: The Home, the Self, and the School,* ed. Joyce L. VanTassel-Baska and Paula Olszewski-Kubilius (New York: Teachers College Press, 1989), 94.

6. J. Galbraith, "8 Great Gripes of the Gifted," *Roeper Review* 7 (1985): 60.

7. John Briggs, *Fire in the Crucible* (Los Angeles: Jeremy P. Tarcher, 1990), 17.

8. Ibid.

9. C. M. Cox, "The Early Mental Traits of 300 Geniuses," *Genetic Studies of Genius*, vol. 2, ed. Lewis Terman (Stanford, Calif.: Stanford University Press, 1926). See also just about anything by Robert J. Steinberg.

10. Doris Wallace, "Giftedness and the Construction of a Creative Life," in *The Gifted and Talented. Developmental Perspectives* (Washington, D.C.: American Psychological Association, 1985), 362.

11. Erich Fromm, *Escape from Freedom* (New York: Avon, 1965), 217.

12. Abraham Maslow, *The Farther Reaches of Human Nature* (New York: Viking, 1971), 184.

13. Briggs, *Fire in the Crucible,* 17.

14. Helen Keller, *My Religion* (New York: Swedenborg Foundation, 1972), 30.

15. Christy Brown, *My Left Foot* (London: Mandarin Books, 1989), 50.

16. Dag Hammarskjöld, *Markings* (New York; Alfred A. Knopf, 1976), 2.

17. Father Bede Griffiths, *The Golden String* (Glasgow: Collins, 1979), 23.

18. Donald Weinstein and Rudolph M. Bell, *Saints and Society* (Chicago: University of Chicago Press, 1982).

19. Ibid., 41.

20. Jill Ker Conway, ed., *Written by Herself: Autobiographies of American Women: An Anthology* (New York: Vintage, 1992), 349.

21. Ibid.

22. Ibid., 349–50.

23. See, for instance, Maslow's discussion of this issue in *The Farther Reaches of Human Nature,* Part 3.

24. Richard Kieckhefer, *Unquiet Souls* (Chicago: University of Chicago Press, 1984), 22.

25. Richard Love interview, *American Art Forum,* KRCB, January 16, 1996.

26. Malcolm X, with the assistance of Alex Haley, *The Autobiography of Malcolm X* (New York: Grove Press, 1964), 100, 386.

27. Eudora Welty, *One Writer's Beginnings* (New York: Warner Books, 1983.

28. Vera John-Steiner, *Notebooks of the Mind: Explorations of Thinking* (Albuquerque: University of New Mexico Press, 1985).

## 8. Wholesome Autonomy

1. Christy Brown, *My Left Foot* (London: Mandarin Books, Octopus Publishing, 1989), 175.

2. Michael Piechowski, "Self-Actualization as a Developmental Structure: A Profile of Antoine de Saint-Exupéry," *Genetic Psychology Monographs,* Department of Educational Psychology, University of Illinois, 1978, 181–242.

3. John Briggs, *Fire in the Crucible* (New York: Jeremy P. Tarcher, 1990), 263.

4. Margaret Mead, "Blackberry Winter: My Earlier Years," in Jill Ker Conway, ed., *Written by Herself: Autobiographies of American Women: An Anthology* (New York: Vintage, 1992), 283, 285.

5. Ibid.

6. Victor Goertzel and Mildred G. Goertzel, *Cradles of Eminence* (Boston: Little, Brown, 1962), 270, 274.

7. Ibid., 257.

8. Ibid.

9. Bruno Bettelheim, *Surviving and Other Essays* (New York: Alfred A. Knopf, 1952), 333–49.

10. Maria Montessori, *Dr. Montessori's Own Handbook* (New York: Schocken Books, 1965), 15.

11. A. H. Maslow, *The Farther Reaches of Human Nature* (New York: An Esalen Book, Viking Press, 1971), 110–11.

12. Bob Geldof with Paul Vallely, *Is That It?* (New York: Ballantine, 1988), 19.

13. Ibid., 19, 22.

14. John Nathan, *Mishima: A Biography* (New York: Little, Brown, 1974), 8.

15. Nathan, *Mishima*, 19. And, for a graphic fictional portrayal of how such an experience might affect a child, read Arthur Golden's *Memoirs of a Geisha* (New York: Vintage Books, 1997).

16. Ibid., x.

17. Ibid., 211.

18. Ibid., 239.

19. John Morse, *Ben Shahn* (New York: Praeger Publishers, 1972), xx.

20. Related to life's meanings, books such as Richard Bolles's lovely, *How to Find Your Mission in Life* (Berkeley, Calif.: Ten Speed Press: 1991) can help us penetrate our own mysterious reason for being and thus find the sense of place and belonging so critical to spiritual vitality.

21. Thomas Merton, *Spiritual Direction and Meditation* (Collegeville, Minn.: Liturgical Press, 1960), 39.

22. Simone Weil, *Two Moral Essays: Draft for a Statement of Human Obligations and Human Personality,* ed. Ronald Hathaway, Pendle Hill Pamphlet no. 240 (Wallingford, Pa.: Pendle Hill Publications, 1991), 17.

23. Morse, *Ben Shahn,* 167.

## 9. Positive Rebellion

1. Gavin De Becker, *Protecting the Gift* (New York: Dial Press, 1999), 168.

2. Alice Miller, *The Drama of the Gifted Child,* trans. Ruth Ward (New York: Basic Books, 1981), 85.

3. Ibid., 98.

4. Robert Lindner, *Prescription for Rebellion* (New York: Grove Press, 1952, 1962), 67.

5. Sandra Cisneros, "Eleven," in *Growing Up Chicano,* ed. Tiffany Ana Lopez (New York: Avon Books, 1993), 157–58.

6. Doris Kearns-Goodwin on *Hardball with Chris Matthews,* July 19, 1999, CNBC, Inc.; transcript prepared by Burrelle's Information Services.

7. Herbert Kohl, *I Won't Learn from You: The Role of Assent in Learning* (Minneapolis: Milkweed Editions, 1991), 10, 20.

8. Helen Keller, *My Religion* (New York: Swedenborg Foundation, 1972).

9. Jean Sulivan, *Morning Sun* (Mahwah, N.J.: Paulist Press, 1988), 63.

10. Leslie Stahl interview, "Experimental Prison," *60 Minutes,* Burrelle's Transcripts, New York, August 30, 1998.

11. "A Confession," in *The Portable Tolstoy,* ed. John Bailey (New York: Penguin Books, 1978), 677–78.

12. Ibid, 672–715.

13. David Essel, M.S., "Silent Teacher" in *Phoenix Soul* (Sarasota, Fla.: Kona Press, 1998), 18.

14. Erich Fromm, *The Art of Loving* (New York: Harper & Row, 1956).

15. *The Confessions of Saint Augustine,* trans. Edward B. Pusey (New York: Collier Macmillan Publishers, 1961), 23–24.

## *10. Early Reconcilers*

1. Michelle Martin, "Church Starts Rebuilding after Fire," *Daily Herald* (Arlington Heights, Ill.), October 30, 1998, 1.

2. Marsha Sinetar, *Living Happily Ever After* (New York: Villard Books, 1990).

3. Marsha Sinetar, *Ordinary People as Monks and Mystics* (Mahwah, N.J.: Paulist Press, 1986).

4. Samuel Osherson, *Finding Our Fathers: The Unfinished Business of Manhood* (New York: Fawcett-Columbine, 1986), 225–28.

5. John Muir, *The Story of My Boyhood and Youth* (San Francisco: Sierra Club Book, 1998), vii, viii.

6. Ibid., ix.

7. Thomas Merton, *The Hidden Ground of Love* (New York: Farrar, Straus, Giroux, 1985), 17.

8. Alice Miller, *The Drama of the Gifted Child* (New York: Basic Books, 1982).

9. Victor and Mildred G. Goertzel, *Cradles of Eminence* (Boston: Little, Brown, 1962), 57.

10. Sebastian Moore, *The Crucified Jesus Is No Stranger* (Mahwah, N.J.: Paulist Press, 1977), 86–87.

## *Epilogue*

1. J. M. Barrie, "Dear Brutus, I," in J. M. and M. J. Cohen, *Penguin Dictionary of Modern Quotations* (Middlesex, England: Penguin Books, 1972), 13:70.

2. Quoted in John Morse, *Ben Shahn* (New York: Praeger Publishers, 1972), 36.

3. St. Teresa of Avila, *Interior Castle,* trans. and ed. E. Allison Peers (Garden City, N.Y.: Doubleday, 1961), 119.

# Index